THE Sun GUIDE 1

EURO 2000

COMPILED BY MARK IRWIN
SOCCER WRITER, *THE SUN*

CollinsWillow
An Imprint of HarperCollins*Publishers*

First published in 2000
by CollinsWillow
an imprint of HarperCollins*Publishers*
London

1   3   5   7   9   8   6   4   2

A CIP catalogue record for this book is available from the British Library

ISBN 0 00 710316 6

Cover and text design by Graeme Andrew

Photographs courtesy of *The Sun* and Allsport

Colour origination by Saxon Photolitho, Norwich

Printed and bound by Scotprint, Musselburgh

The HarperCollins website address is
www.**fire**and**water**.com

Picture credits
Allsport: 3, 6-7, 12, 13, 44-45, 47-49, 51, 52 (inset), 53 (c and br), 54, 55, 56, 57 (br),
58, 59, 60, 61, 62-63, 64-65, 66, 67 (main), 68, 70, 72, 73, 75, 78 (b), 79, 80-83, 92, 93 (b),
94-99, 101 (b), 102-103, 106, 107 (l), 108 (br), 109, 113 (l), 114, 116 (b), 117 (b), 120,
121, 122-127

Hulton Getty: 88, 89, 90, 93 (t), 107 (r), 111, 113 (r), 116 (t), 117 (t)

News International Newspapers: 1, 4, 5 (both) 8, 9, 10, 11, 14-43, 46, 50 (both), 52 (main),
53 (tr), 55 (tr), 57, 58 (tr), 59 (inset), 61 (tr), 67, 69, 71, 72 (br), 74, 76-77, 78 (t), 84-87, 100,
101 (t), 104-105, 108 (tl), 110 (l), 115, 118

Mirror Syndication: 110 (r), 112

*The team squads for Euro 2000 were not due to be named until some time after this book
went to press. As such there has been a certain amount of crystal-ball gazing in so far as
participating countries' squad members are concerned. The cut-off deadline for information
appearing in this book was 13 March 2000, and unless otherwise stated all statistics and
squad profiles have been provided up to that date.*

CONTENTS

INTRODUCTION...........................6

FEATURE BY JOHN SADLER
King Kev Can Rule Europe.........8

ENGLAND PLAYER PROFILES

Tony Adams 14

David Batty 16

David Beckham 17

Nicky Butt 19

Sol Campbell 20

Andy Cole 22

Rio Ferdinand 23

Robbie Fowler 24

Martin Keown 25

Graeme Le Saux 26

Nigel Martyn 27

Steve McManaman 28

Gary Neville 29

Phil Neville 30

Michael Owen 31

Ray Parlour 33

Kevin Phillips 34

Jamie Redknapp 35

David Seaman 36

Paul Scholes 38

Alan Shearer 39

Tim Sherwood 41

Gareth Southgate 42

Ian Walker 43

LATE ON THE SCENE
Emile Heskey, Jason Wilcox,
Dennis Wise, Richard Wright 44

FEATURE BY STEVEN HOWARD
England v Germany:
It's Always The Germans 48

TEAM PREVIEWS

Germany 52

Portugal 54

Romania 55

EURO 2000 QUALIFIERS 73

HISTORY OF THE EUROPEAN CHAMPIONSHIPS 88

FEATURE BY BRIAN WOOLNOUGH
Five Memorable Matches 102

ALL-TIME GREATS......................106

DID YOU KNOW ?.........................118

EURO 2000 VENUES 122

TOURNAMENT PLANNER 128

Italy 56

Belgium 58

Sweden 59

Turkey 60

Norway 61

Spain 62

Slovenia 64

Yugoslavia 65

Czech Republic 66

France 68

Holland 70

Denmark 72

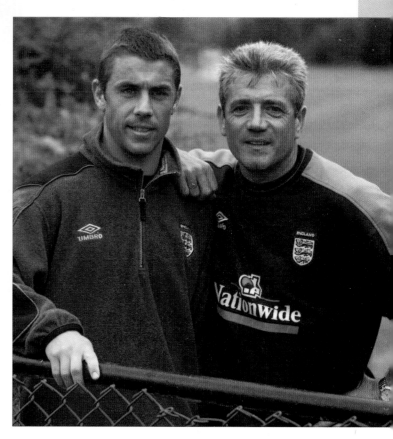

INTRODUCTION

by Paul Ridley, Head of Sport, *The Sun*

Here we go again. It's us against the Germans. It is always us against the Germans. And don't mention the penalties. The threat to all Kevin Keegan's hopes and dreams is a real one. Former England coach Terry Venables was once asked what he most admired about Germany. 'Their results,' he replied. And not a hint of that famous grin.

Can Keegan give us something to smile about this time? We've been the nearly men and, more often than not, the nowhere near it men, since 1966. That's a desperately poor return for a nation of football lovers who will set up camp in front of the television on Saturday 10 June and only emerge into the summer sunlight after it is all over on Sunday 2 July.

Keegan's troops are not short of guts, experience — or talent. Tony Adams and Alan Shearer epitomise the spirit of the side. David Beckham can dominate. Sol Campbell can come of age. We are safe in the hands of David Seaman and Nigel Martyn. And a previously unsung hero will step forward and win our hearts. Kevin Phillips, maybe. Or Ray Parlour.

The Sun's team of top soccer writers, reporters and photographers will be at every match to capture the action in words and pictures. This guide puts the facts at your fingertips and will add to your enjoyment of Euro 2000.

Keegan must weld his squad into a cohesive fighting unit. Bring on the Portuguese, the Italians, the Dutch. Keegan will pump up his men and send them out to war.

Sixteen teams line-up. One side will believe in themselves more than the rest. That will prove the difference. Keegan is capable of instilling that all-consuming belief into his lionhearts.

We will all be urging them on to the final in Rotterdam. Just don't think about the Germans ... or the penalties.

KING KEV CAN RULE EUROPE

by John Sadler, Sports columnist, *The Sun*

There is something endearing, something magical in the personality and working techniques of Kevin Keegan that separates him from his contemporaries in the vicious, often unfair, world of football management. The child still lurks within many of them. But with the 49-year-old Yorkshireman the gloriously innocent optimism of youth remains so close to the surface that it often breaks right through his skin.

His regard for the game, the enthusiasm that burned inside him as a kid endlessly chasing a ball around a green oasis called the Bullring in the mining district of Balby near Doncaster, has remained undoused by the pressures of the modern game that have extinguished more vulnerable men.

This, remember, is the club manager who once analysed the job of the England manager — long before any notion that he would eventually fill the post — and said: 'I honestly believe it is his responsibility to excite and entertain all those people who pay to watch the international side at Wembley.'

> 'When I look at the individual players in the England set-up I just know the other managers taking teams to the finals will be looking at us and saying "Wow!" '

No allowance, there, for the reality that such ideal philosophy could be so easily suffocated by visiting teams whose sole object and ambition was the avoidance of defeat. For Kevin Keegan, the priority of any footballer and any football team should be to excite the paying customer and leave him, or her, content in the belief they had been offered genuine value for their money.

BRIGHT FUTURE... Keegan's hopes rest with the talents of Michael Owen.

FACE THE MUSIC...
Keegan, unlike
Glenn Hoddle,
has always had the
media on his side.

Some will call it naive. And they are the ones who don't call it impossible. But Keegan provides living proof that the impossible is achievable. He made an outstanding footballer of himself — from an unspectacular, if not ordinary, natural talent.

He carried the back-street, playground, childhood fantasies of his early years into an obsessive determination to break down every barrier that obstructed his path to the highest levels of the game. He was to play with that same gratitude, unquenchable spirit and sheer joy that told the world it was great to be alive and kicking ... kicking a ball for a handsome living and lasting fame in Liverpool, Hamburg, Southampton and Newcastle. As well as in most corners of the world with England, many times as captain of his country.

In a sense, the medals that jangled in his pocket along the way were of secondary importance to the satisfaction of simply playing with, and against, the best performers on earth. It is precisely that child-like thrill and feeling of privilege to be earning his living from a mere game that brought him fame and fortune, which has Keegan looking ahead to the Euro 2000 championship in Holland and Belgium with such optimism. 'When I look at the individual players in the England set up,' he says, 'I just know the other managers taking teams to the finals will be looking at us as well and saying "Wow!" '

Curiously, I was born not a dozen miles from the place where Keegan drew his first breath though his 'debut' was 11 years later than mine. Yet I was not to know him until his later days as an England player — then, more closely, when he took to management with such style and success on Tyneside. If ever a journalist feels the need to have his enthusiasm freshened, the threat of cynicism chased away, then I recommend an hour or so in Keegan's company. I can vouch for the infectious optimism, the sparkle in his eyes, the ability to transfer the conviction that something good can

be fashioned from the most disheartening of circumstances.

His admiration for the extraordinary talent of the leading players, his unshakeable confidence in those at his disposal, his mistrust of those who betray their

If ever a journalist feels the need to have his enthusiasm freshened, the threat of cynicism chased away, then I recommend an hour or so in Keegan's company.

ability, his unswerving commitment to the creation of a team that entertains and wins ...

It is no surprise to me that the England players under his command speak openly and gratefully about a spirit and bond between squad and manager that is stronger and healthier than any in recent memory.

When judgment day comes, whether it be at the end of England's Euro 2000 challenge or their forthcoming World Cup qualifying campaign, Keegan will be among the sternest adjudicators. He is not averse to severe self-analysis.

People who scoff, the know-nothings who claim he ups and runs at the first sign of flak, conveniently forget the frankness of his reaction to England's somewhat fortunate squeak into the European finals by way of that play-off against Scotland, ending with embarrassment at Wembley.

How many managers have read the papers, scanned the brutal headlines, heard the misgivings of the television pundits and admitted: 'I have to say that 99 per cent of the criticism was justified. We have a lot of improving to do.'

Talk to him now, though, and the attitude is that of a manager who knows that the past cannot be changed — like a child who believes

PRACTICE MAKES PERFECT...
Above and opposite:
The England manager enjoys
the rough and tumble of the
training ground.

JUST LIKE THAT!...Keegan knows a thing or two about scoring for his country.

every tomorrow will be a brighter, better day. He thinks England have an excellent chance, not of making a decent show at Euro 2000 but of winning it. Providing, that is, his team can overcome the distinctly awkward challenge of Portugal, their first opponents, in Eindhoven on 12 June

Keegan looks no further than that, saying: 'When the draw was made, people gasped as England were paired with Germany. When we drew them again in the World Cup qualifiers, they gasped again and laughed. All the talk, since, has been about the Germans and our recent match history against them. The close encounters, the penalty shoot-outs, the bad luck. I knew, instantly, that the Portugal game was and remains the one that needs our total concentration. Experience, both as a player and manager, tells me that a good start is vital in any competition. If we get off to a flyer, if we beat the Portuguese, the whole mood of the squad and the country will be upbeat and expectant.

'I have to take the broad view, I know, but in the run-up to the finals the emphasis will be on the Portugal game. I don't think any horse that fell badly at the first fence ever won the Grand National. Not that defeat would put us out — but victory would

substantially reduce the odds against it.' Keegan, of course, made an unorthodox start to his career in charge of the England side. But, once more, that boyish fascination and thrill soon told him he would need to shed the part-time arrangement and get stuck into it on a permanent basis.

KEEGAN FACT FILE

BIRTH DATE AND PLACE: 14 February 1951, Doncaster

CLUBS: Scunthorpe (124 lg apps/18 lg goals), Liverpool (230/68), Hamburg (90/32), Southampton (68/37), Newcastle (78/48)

INTERNATIONAL APPEARANCES: 63/21 goals

MANAGERIAL EXPERIENCE: Newcastle (February 1992–January 1997), Fulham (December 1998-June 1999)

RECORD AS NEWCASTLE MANAGER (League only):

91-92	P16	W7	D2	L7	F23	A25
92-93	P46	W29	D9	L8	F92	A38
93-94	P42	W 23	D8	L11	F 82	A 41
94-95	P42	W20	D12	L10	F67	A47
95-96	P38	W24	D6	L8	F66	A37
96-97	P38	W19	D11	L8	F73	A40

RECORD AS FULHAM MANAGER

97-98 Play-offs	P2	W0	D1	L1	F1	A2
98-99	P46	W31	D8	L7	F79	A32

He reflects, now, and admits: 'It took me six months to begin to understand what the job is all about. Now, six or eight months after going full-time, I have a much better grasp and appreciation of the demands. After warm-up matches with Argentina and Brazil I know I need to pay close attention to the friendly against the Ukraine, the last game an England side will play at the old Wembley stadium. But it's not only the match.

[Keegan] thinks England have an excellent chance, not of making a decent show at Euro 2000, but of winning it.

'Following that fixture on 31 May I have to announce my chosen squad of 22 players for the finals. I have to reduce it from 35. That is a vital decision. Having made it I will use the game in Malta to give most of the squad a run out.'

So each of his players will wear the shirt before moving into the training camp for the real thing. They will be given the taste that already has Keegan licking his lips and dreaming. He almost leaps from his chair when he says: 'I am so excited by it all. Sure, we struggled to qualify, turned in some poor performances as well as some better ones and hardly finished on a high-note against Scotland at home.

'But none of that matters any more. What's gone is gone. All the pessimistic talk has gone out of the window. The Czech Republic qualified by getting 30 points from their 10 games but they don't arrive at the finals with any better chance than us.

'It's a level playing field as they say, even though we scrambled through. I don't think we have reason to fear any of the opposition. What I do know is that the team who win Euro 2000 will not only need to play well but will require some luck as well. Anybody who smirks at that has only to remember Manchester United and how they won the European Cup against Bayern Munich!'

The mid-winter months have frustrated Keegan. The reality of the England job, the lack of close and regular contact with his players, has weighed heavily on the little man who loves nothing more than the rough and tumble of training ground activity and banter of the dressing room.

'What I am really looking forward to,' he says, 'is getting together with the players for a period of time. That happens so infrequently, only at major

FALLEN GREAT... Swapping shirts with a young Diego Maradona.

tournaments. The benefit of that will show the rest of Europe what we are made of.'

It reduces the chance of excuse, of course. In the event of failure there can be no complaint about lack of necessary preparation and understanding of the manager's requirements and the players' ability to fulfill them. Keegan goes even further, confessing: 'There can be no excuses this time. We will be into a training camp after friendlies against good quality opposition. We will be as well-prepared as any nation in the championship.

'Personally, I can't wait for the real thing to start. I don't contemplate things going wrong. I don't consider defeat. I think about beating Portugal, getting better all the time and of ending the tournament as champions of Europe.

'What a prospect! Then we could set about qualifying for the World Cup with terrific confidence, yes, thinking about that other match against Germany. Who wouldn't get excited about a future like that?'

You don't contradict. You recognise the wonderful, wide-eyed optimism of the child within the man. And look forward to joining him on his roller-coaster ride.

Tony Adams

Leader of the pack

CLUB: Arsenal
PREVIOUS CLUBS: None
BIRTH DATE/PLACE: 10 October 1966
Romford, Essex
HEIGHT/WEIGHT: 6ft 3in/13st 11lb
ENGLAND DEBUT: 18 February 1987 v Spain
(Madrid, won 4-2)
ENGLAND APPEARANCES: 62 (4 goals)

'We were the best team at Euro 96 and should have won it. The country looks at the quality in our squad and expects us to win something.'

Tony Adams is a winner. Near misses mean nothing to him. He is only interested in first place. The man who has led Arsenal's Championship challenges for the past 15 years has achieved just about every domestic honour going during a remarkable one-club career at Highbury. Yet at international level, he remains unfulfilled. And time is running out for him. Realistically, Euro 2000 is Adams' last shot at gaining that elusive winners' medal with England. His body is starting to feel the effects of one war too many.

Yet the drive and desire of this remarkable competitor will not diminish until he has reached his goal. Which means no member of Kevin Keegan's team will be more motivated for action this summer against Portugal, Romania and, particularly, Germany.

He remains a complete professional, as committed today as the day he first broke into the Arsenal side back in the 1983-84 season. Yet he has enjoyed a new lease of life since Arsene Wenger was appointed Arsenal's coach in 1996. The Frenchman's meticulous attention to diet, preparation and flexibility has added years to Adams' career. The towering defender is no longer under such intense pressure to push his body through the pain barrier and squeeze out one more game for the Arsenal cause.

Since his days as a teenaged rookie learning his trade from David O'Leary, Adams has managed more than 700 first-team performances for the club he joined from school and has never even contemplated leaving. He has been the mainstay of a legendary back four which set new standards in defensive excellence. With Steve Bould, Lee Dixon and Nigel Winterburn alongside him, Arsenal conceded just 18 goals in 38 league games when they won the Championship in 1991.

Adams has been part of three Championship-winning teams, collected two FA Cups, two League Cups and the European Cup-Winners' Cup. So it was hardly a surprise when Manchester United boss Alex Ferguson recently admitted that if he could have brought any one player of the last ten years to Old Trafford, it would have been Tony Adams.

Realistically, Euro 2000 is Adams' last shot at gaining that elusive winners' medal with England.

Fortunately for England, Kevin Keegan can call on the services of the Arsenal ace whenever it suits him. True, Adams' England appearances have become more infrequent in recent years due to an accumulation of injuries. But he is always there when it matters. And this summer, it really matters.

David Batty

Beware of the Bitey

CLUB: Leeds
PREVIOUS CLUBS: Leeds, Blackburn, Newcastle (joined Leeds in December 1998 for £4.5 million).
BIRTH DATE/PLACE: 2 December 1968, Leeds
HEIGHT/WEIGHT: 5ft 8in/11st 10lb
ENGLAND DEBUT: 21 May 1991 v USSR as substitute (Wembley, won 3-1)
ENGLAND APPEARANCES: 42 (0 goals)

'When I look at the players in our squad, the quality of the guys we have in the team, then I know we can beat anyone if we get the ball into the last third of the pitch.'

Born and bred in the shadow of Elland Road, David Batty was hailed by Leeds United's long-suffering supporters as the man to fill the void left by former idol Billy Bremner.

It seemed inconceivable at the time that he would ever wear any other team's shirt, yet when Leeds' ambition to build on their shock Championship success in 1991 failed to match his own, he didn't think twice about moving to Blackburn in a £2.5 million deal. Within 18 months of his arrival at Ewood Park, Rovers were also crowned kings of the Premiership. Yet when things started to go pear-shaped the following year, he was off on his travels again.

It was Kevin Keegan who finally lured him to Newcastle in March 1996, but the rot had already set in at St James' Park. The writing was on for the wall for Batty the moment that Ruud Gullit took charge in August 1998. Within four months he was heading back to Leeds and his first love.

For England, Batty has taken over from Paul Ince as his country's first choice ball winner.

For England, Batty has taken over from Paul Ince as his country's first choice ball winner. He dislikes his image as an aggressor who simply does the donkey work for more gifted team-mates and believes he has never received true credit for his passing and vision.

Fortunately for Batty, Keegan appreciates his true worth. He did, after all, once pay £3.75 million for him when he was Newcastle boss. At Euro 2000, a fit and rested David Batty could be priceless.

David Beckham

Let the genius loose…

CLUB: Manchester United
PREVIOUS CLUBS: None
BIRTH DATE/PLACE: 2 May 1975, Leytonstone East London
HEIGHT/WEIGHT: 6ft/11st 9lb
ENGLAND DEBUT: 1 September 1996 v Moldova (Chisinau, won 3-0).
ENGLAND APPEARANCES: 28 (1 goal)

'I know I'm expected to pull myself to a new higher level every time I play; I accept that because that's what I want to do, to perform at the highest level.'

No player at Euro 2000 will be under greater scrutiny than David Beckham. The Manchester United midfielder has developed from multi-talented footballer into a one-man media circus over the past couple of years. In the next few weeks his every move will be photographed, filmed and analysed. Daily news bulletins will keep the world up to date on the state of Beckham's moods, his appearance, his haircut and even his tattoo.

Of course, this is no everyday footballer we're talking about. For David Beckham is one half of arguably the world's foremost 'celebrity couple'. Beckham's marriage to Victoria 'Posh Spice' Adams catapulted him to a whole new level of stardom. His efforts on the football pitch are almost incidental for many of his closest observers…unless he blows a fuse again. And that will be Kevin Keegan's greatest fear on the eve of the Championships which will make or break him as a coach.

There is little doubt that a fit and focused David Beckham will be England's greatest asset at Euro 2000. No player in the world crosses the ball better than the United wide-man. Few can deliver free-kicks with such venom, power and accuracy. But behind the world-class talent lies a fragile temperament which will be tested to the limit and beyond in the coming months. For David Beckham now has a reputation as a man snapping under the strain. And opponents will do anything they can to push him over the edge.

Nobody will ever forget Beckham's retaliatory kick at Argentina's Diego Simeone during the last World Cup in France. His brief act of petulance cost him a red card and, ultimately, the wrath of a nation as ten man England were booted out of the tournament on penalties.

Eighteen months on and he was off again, this time for an horrendous challenge on a Mexican opponent during the otherwise meaningless World Club Championships in Rio. In between those dismissals were a series of disciplinary near misses, obscene gestures to rival supporters baiting him over his private life as well as needless, off the ball swipes at his rivals.

There is little doubt that a fit and focused David Beckham will be England's greatest asset at Euro 2000.

Keegan knows that what Beckham might get away with in the Premiership will not go unpunished at Euro 2000. He will do everything he can to protect his brightest star, who celebrates his 25th birthday a month before England's opening Euro 2000 game against Portugal. Yet even Manchester United boss Sir Alex Ferguson has admitted he can no longer control the Beckham bandwagon despite all his efforts to keep his charge under wraps, because so much of the attention focused on Beckham is totally self-inflicted.

It is almost as if he goes out of his way to get his picture in the paper wearing a dress, a hanky on his head or a £40,000 diamond crucifix.

There is no doubt that opponents respect him for

what he has achieved at club level, particularly his role in helping United past Barcelona, Inter Milan, Juventus and Bayern Munich to win the Champions' League last year.

But there is a huge difference between respect and fear and Beckham now has to justify the hype and prove he belongs among the true greats of the game. He will never have a better chance to write his name in football folklore... and not just as a man who wore strange clothes.

Nicky Butt

The Ginger Ninja

CLUB: Manchester United
PREVIOUS CLUBS: None
BIRTH DATE/PLACE: 21 January 1975, Manchester
HEIGHT/WEIGHT: 5ft 10in/11st 5lb
ENGLAND DEBUT: 29 March 1997 v Mexico as substitute (Wembley, won 2-0)
ENGLAND APPEARANCES: 8 (0 goals)

'I realise that most people regard me as a ball-winner, but I think there is a lot more to my game than just making tackles.'

Angel-faced Nicky Butt might look as though butter wouldn't melt in his mouth, but there is a real bite to his challenge. He has never pulled out of a tackle in his life and competes for every ball as though it was his last.

When team-mate Roy Keane was suspended from last year's European Cup final, Butt was considered so vital by Alex Ferguson that he was left out of United's FA Cup final team to protect him from possible injury. Even when United's local hero was sent-off in successive matches against Barcelona and Arsenal in June 1998, Fergie refused to utter a single word of condemnation. For though Butt may have graduated in the Old Trafford shadows of Beckham, Giggs and the Neville brothers, his contribution to the club's success has been every bit as important.

At the age of just 25, he is already a veteran of six Champions' League campaigns. Incredibly, he has played more European games than any other player in United's illustrious history. That experience could prove invaluable to England at Euro 2000.

As long as there is a tackle to be made, there will always be a place for Nicky Butt.

His first four caps were all won as a substitute and he has yet to start in a competitive match for his country. Yet his place in Keegan's squad is assured. As long as there is a tackle to be made, there will always be a place for Nicky Butt.

Sol Campbell

The big man is ready

CLUB: Tottenham Hotspur
PREVIOUS CLUBS: None
BIRTH DATE/PLACE: 18 September 1974, Stratford, NE London
HEIGHT/WEIGHT: 6ft 2in/14st 4lb
ENGLAND DEBUT: 18 May 1996 v Hungary as substitute (Wembley, won 3-0)
ENGLAND APPEARANCES: 30 (0 goals)

'I've always felt that central defence is my best position because that is where I play for my club. But if the England manager asks me to play a different role, I'm not going to argue with him.'

Sol Campbell's dilemma is that he is just too damn versatile for his own good. Whenever England are facing a defensive problem, the 25-year-old powerhouse is the man they always send for.

In the Euro 2000 play-offs, the left-footed giant was asked to play as emergency right-back to fill the gap created by the injured Gary Neville. In the first leg of the clash with Scotland, Campbell didn't put a foot wrong as England cruised to a 2-0 victory at Hampden Park.

Unfortunately for Campbell, he was so good that day in Glasgow that people forgot he was playing completely out of position. So when he was given a chasing by Scotland wide-man Neil McCann in the return match at Wembley four days later, England fans were genuinely shocked by Sol's vulnerability.

Campbell, though, remained characteristically unruffled. He knows that Kevin Keegan is not looking at him as his long-term right-back. Nor will his international prospects have suffered as a result of one below-par performance. For the lightning-quick Campbell is used to coping with big expectations.

Since his days as a 14-year-old schoolboy at the FA's School of Excellence at Lilleshall, he has always been singled out as a player to watch. At 17 he helped England win the European Youth Championships. He scored on his Spurs debut against Chelsea when sent on as a striker two months after his 18th birthday. Within months he was Tottenham's regular left-back, making occasional appearances in midfield, before being told to concentrate his efforts on central defence.

The lightning-quick Campbell is used to coping with big expectations.

Terry Venables' appointment as England coach in January 1994 accelerated Campbell's international promotion. Although he didn't contribute to England's Euro 96 campaign, the experience he gained as a member of Venables' squad stood him in good stead for France 98, when he cemented his reputation as one of the finest young defenders in the world.

Now he is one of the most coveted players in Europe. With his Spurs contract due to expire in 2001, every ambitious club in England, Italy and Spain are monitoring his situation. Manchester United regard him as the perfect partner for Jaap Stam and can offer him regular Champions' League football and more money than he would know what to do with.

But the Sol Man will just take it all in his stride. The king of cool is in complete control as usual.

Andy Cole
Fired up

CLUB: Manchester United
PREVIOUS CLUBS: Arsenal, Bristol City, Newcastle
(joined United in January 1995 for £7 million)
BIRTH DATE/PLACE: 15 October 1971, Nottingham
HEIGHT/WEIGHT: 5ft 10in/12st 4lb
ENGLAND DEBUT: 29 March 1995 v Uruguay as
substitute (Wembley, 0-0)
ENGLAND APPEARANCES: 7 (0 goals)

> '**I have the utmost respect for Kevin Keegan. He gave me my chance in the big time and told me to enjoy myself. He helped me relax and made me into a better player.**'

Andy Cole is a man who is used to ruffling feathers. He fell out irrevocably with former England boss Glenn Hoddle, furiously speaking his mind when Hoddle suggested he was not good enough for international football. Even Kevin Keegan had to have a quiet word with his petulant protege last year when Cole used his autobiography to criticise Alan Shearer's unchallenged England position.

Keegan's advice has helped Cole finally come to terms with his position in the international pecking order and he will travel to Euro 2000 with no loftier ambitions than a place on the bench. Yet that does not mean he has suddenly developed a lower opinion of his talent. And in light of his recent achievements with Manchester United, that is hardly surprising.

When Alex Ferguson smashed the British transfer record to prise Cole from Keegan's grasp at Newcastle, Geordie fans were distraught. Yet within a year they were chuckling to themselves as Cole was unable to maintain his phenomenal scoring record at Old Trafford. Only Ferguson refused to concede that he had made a rare mistake in the transfer market.

The arrival of £12.6 million Dwight Yorke at the start of the 1998-99 campaign proved the turning point in Cole's United career. From then on, his international claims could no longer be overlooked.

Keegan's advice has helped Cole finally come to terms with his position in the international pecking order.

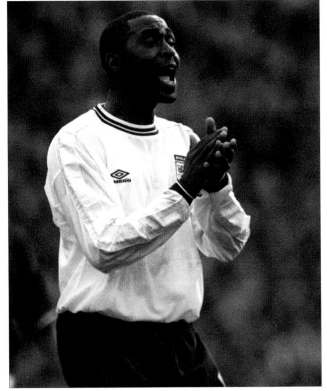

Rio Ferdinand

Lion heart

CLUB: West Ham
PREVIOUS CLUBS: None
BIRTH DATE/PLACE: 8 November 1978,
Peckham, London
HEIGHT/WEIGHT: 6ft 2in/12st
ENGLAND DEBUT: 15 November 1997 v Cameroon
as substitute (Wembley, won 2-0)
ENGLAND APPEARANCES: 9 (0 goals)

'There is nothing like pulling on that white shirt and seeing the three lions on your chest. That's what you dream about on your estate as a kid.'

Peckham-born Rio was always going to make it big, right from the moment he was asked to train with England's Euro 96 squad after just one game for West Ham. The ball-playing defender had already been compared to Upton Park legend Bobby Moore by Hammers boss Harry Redknapp.

Glenn Hoddle, waiting patiently in the wings to take over from Terry Venables, carefully noted Ferdinand's calm composure during those European Championship preparations. Little more than a year after taking charge, Hoddle called Rio into his squad for the game against Moldova, then publicly and humiliatingly ditched him when the kid was convicted of drink-driving in the week of the Princess of Wales' death.

Such an experience would have destroyed most youngsters. But Ferdinand proved his character by ignoring the controversy and continuing to silence Premiership strikers for West Ham. His calm authority on the ball, his speed of reaction and impeccable reading of the game meant that Hoddle could not continue to ignore the lad. In November 1997 he became the fourth youngest player to play for England this century when he replaced Gareth Southgate during a 2-0 Wembley win over the Cameroons.

Rio remains a key figure in England's future plans.

Even though he did not play at France 98 and managed only a couple of appearances during the Euro 2000 qualifying campaign, Rio remains a key figure in England's future plans.

Robbie Fowler

Natural born thriller

CLUB: Liverpool
PREVIOUS CLUBS: None
BIRTH DATE/PLACE: 9 April 1975, Toxteth, Liverpool
HEIGHT/WEIGHT: 5ft 11in/11st 10lb
ENGLAND DEBUT: 27 March 1996 v Bulgaria as substitute (Wembley, won 1-0)
ENGLAND APPEARANCES: 11 (2 goals)

> 'There is always a lot of expectancy on the strikers and I know I still haven't proved myself at England level.'

Kevin Keegan believes Robbie Fowler could be his secret weapon at Euro 2000. The Liverpool striker is still finding his way back to form and fitness following an ankle operation at the start of the year. But Keegan is convinced that the 25-year-old Scouser is the most natural goalscorer at his disposal.

In a stop-start international career stretching back more than four years, Fowler had not made two successive starts for his country until last September.

He managed only a couple of brief substitute appearances during Euro 96 and didn't even make the final squad for the last World Cup finals because of injury.

> **Keegan is convinced that the 25-year-old Scouser is the most natural goalscorer at his disposal.**

Fowler became the youngest player in Liverpool history to score 150 goals for the club last season. He burst onto the scene with a bang, scoring five goals in only his fourth game for Liverpool in a 1993 League Cup tie at Fulham. A boyhood Evertonian who was a part of England's European Youth-championship winning side, he was named the PFA's Young Footballer of the Year in both 1994/95 and 1995/96.

His career has been overshadowed by controversy. But Fowler has made a conscious effort to improve his image in recent months and knows he is in danger of failing to fully exploit his incredible talent. A decent Euro 2000 would go a long way towards making up for lost time.

Martin Keown

My time has come

CLUB: Arsenal
PREVIOUS CLUBS: Arsenal, Aston Villa, Everton
(rejoined Arsenal in February 1993 for £2 million)
BIRTH DATE/PLACE: 24 July 1966, Oxford
HEIGHT/WEIGHT: 6ft 1in/12st 4lb
ENGLAND DEBUT: 19 February 1992 v France
(Wembley, won 2-0)
ENGLAND APPEARANCES: 28 (1 goal)

'It has taken me a long time to reach these heights, but now I feel ready to play at this level.'

Martin Keown has never been a player who lacked self-belief. Now, at the age of 33, he has finally convinced the rest of football to share that confidence in his defensive abilities.

The Arsenal stopper — tough as old boots and twice as durable — has had to bide his time and bite his lip to gain recognition as the best man-marker in the English game. Groomed alongside Tony Adams in the Arsenal youth team, he walked out of Highbury after just half a season in their first team because new manager George Graham wouldn't meet his contract demands.

Keown has always maintained that he does not regret his seven years away from Arsenal. It was while at Everton that he won his first ten caps for England. Yet it wasn't until he returned to Highbury and Bruce Rioch took over from Graham that Keown really began to show his true qualities. Encouraged to control and pass the ball by the new

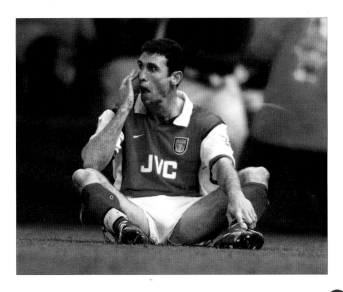

Keown has had to bide his time and bite his lip to gain recognition as the best man-marker in the English game.

Arsenal boss, Keown was voted Arsenal's Player of the Year in 1995.

Even then his contribution was still overlooked by many observers. Only when Glenn Hoddle recalled him to England duty after a four-year absence did Keown's critics realise that here was a top-class player in his own right, not just an effective partner for the more feted Adams. Now he is virtually indispensable for England, playing a greater part in the Euro 2000 qualifying campaign than any other defender.

Graeme Le Saux

It's all about timing

CLUB: Chelsea
PREVIOUS CLUBS: Chelsea, Blackburn (rejoined Chelsea in August 1997 for £5 million)
BIRTH DATE/PLACE: 17 October 1968, Jersey
HEIGHT/WEIGHT: 5ft 10in/11st 9lb
ENGLAND DEBUT: 9 March 1994 v Denmark as substitute (Wembley, won 1-0)
ENGLAND APPEARANCES: 35 (1 goal)

'It has been a difficult season for me because of my injury problems, but having the opportunity to claim a place in a European Championship squad was a great motivator to get my fitness back.'

Jersey-born Graeme Le Saux is relishing life back at cosmopolitan Chelsea after a spell at Blackburn which brought him a League Championship medal in 1995 and the notoriety of his Champions' League punch-up with team-mate David Batty the following season.

It was Chelsea's scouts who discovered the schoolboy Le Saux, playing for the Jersey club St Pauls. He quickly settled at the London club

and looked destined for great things when he scored on his League debut shortly after his 21st birthday. But the constant managerial changes at Stamford Bridge left Le Saux in a state of uncertainty, constantly switched from defence to midfield and back again.

It was only when he moved to Ewood Park for a mere £750,000 that he was allowed by new boss Kenny Dalglish to concentrate all his efforts into developing as a left-back.

Within months of his move, his progress was

It was Chelsea's scouts who discovered the schoolboy Le Saux, playing for the Jersey club St Pauls.

rewarded with an England call-up from new international coach Terry Venables and only a broken ankle prevented him from participating at Euro 96.

An ever-present during the 1998 World Cup finals, Le Saux played in just two of Kevin Keegan's first nine games in charge because of injury. His absence was sorely felt as England experimented with a whole series of left-sided defenders and stumbled towards Euro 2000 qualification.

Le Saux's return to action from injury might have come too late to rescue Chelsea's Championship challenge, but it could prove perfect for England.

Nigel Martyn

Handy to have around

CLUB: Leeds
PREVIOUS CLUBS: Bristol Rovers, Crystal Palace
(joined Leeds in July 1996 for £2.2 million)
BIRTH DATE/PLACE: 11 August 1966, St.Austell
HEIGHT/WEIGHT: 6ft 2in/14st 10lb
ENGLAND DEBUT: 29 April 1992 v CIS as
substitute (Moscow, 2-2)
ENGLAND APPEARANCES: 12

'Things have worked out really well for me at Leeds and being part of a successful club side has helped to revive my international career. I don't think I've let anyone down whenever I've played for England.'

When David Seaman was ruled out by injury for England's final Euro 2000 qualifiers against Luxembourg and Poland last September, coach Kevin Keegan didn't even give a second thought about turning to Nigel Martyn.

Predictably, the ever-reliable Leeds keeper didn't let anyone down, keeping a clean sheet at Wembley and then pulling off a couple of vital saves in Warsaw to earn England a priceless lifeline.

Even when he was axed to make way for Seaman's play-off return, the unassuming Cornishman never uttered a word of complaint. After four and a half years in the international wilderness, he is just making the most of his England renaissance.

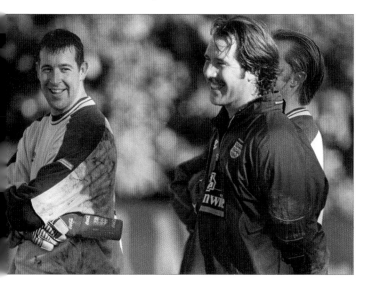

After four and a half years in the international wilderness, he is just making the most of his England renaissance.

He appeared to be on the brink of great things when he forced his way into Graham Taylor's team in 1992. But after just three brief appearances, he inexplicably disappeared without trace. It was only after a high profile move to Leeds in the summer of 1996 that Martyn was able to attract the headlines he needed to boost his claim. He has since enjoyed a new lease of life at Elland Road, playing behind the exciting young team being assembled by David O'Leary.

Steve McManaman

Give us a cracker, Macca

CLUB: Real Madrid
PREVIOUS CLUBS: Liverpool (joined Real in July 1999 as a free agent)
BIRTH DATE/PLACE: 11 February 1972, Liverpool
HEIGHT/WEIGHT: 6ft/10st 6lb
ENGLAND DEBUT: 16 November 1994 v Nigeria as substitute (Wembley, won 1-0)
ENGLAND APPEARANCES: 26 (2 goals)

'There is still more to come from me internationally. I know I have my critics, but I want to achieve so much with England.'

Six years after winning his first England cap, Steve McManaman has still to convince the country that he fully deserves his place in the international squad.

No one doubts McManaman's talent. On his day, he is one of the most exciting wide men in the world, a player able to beat defenders at will to deliver a killer pass. Unfortunately for McManaman, his day does not seem to come often enough.

Only Terry Venables really knew how to coax the best out of McManaman on a regular basis. During Euro 96, McManaman was a constant threat against the best defenders in Europe until England lost to Germany on penalties in the semi-finals.

Although Glenn Hoddle took the player to the last

World Cup, he only gave McManaman 17 minutes of action as a late substitute for Paul Scholes in the first round match against Colombia.

Kevin Keegan has done everything he can to revive McManaman's England career.

Kevin Keegan has done everything he can to revive McManaman's England career. Two goals against Luxembourg last September — his first for his country in 25 games — suggested that the player had finally taken up the challenge. But a dismal performance in the goalless draw in Poland four days later proved it was yet another false dawn.

If Steve McManaman ever learns how to turn on the talent every week he will be a world-beater. That is why he remains a part of England's plans.

Gary Neville

Winning is a habit

CLUB: Manchester United
PREVIOUS CLUBS: None
BIRTH DATE/PLACE: 18 February 1975, Bury
HEIGHT/WEIGHT: 5ft 11in/12st 7lb
ENGLAND DEBUT: 3 June 1995 v Japan
(Wembley, won 2-1)
ENGLAND APPEARANCES: 34 (0 goals)

'I have been lucky enough to play for some of the greatest managers in football. But at international level, it doesn't matter who is in the dug out. The people of England are your manager in those games.'

They say in football that winning becomes a habit. If that is true, Gary Neville developed the habit at a very young age. One of the first graduates of Alex Ferguson's meticulously planned youth policy at Manchester United, right-back Neville has known nothing but success throughout his career.

His very first appearance for United's senior team came on the day they were presented with the League Championship trophy in 1994. Although his one-match contribution wasn't enough to win him a medal that year, he has more than earned the three title triumphs that have subsequently followed at Old Trafford.

When United ended their 31-year wait for the European Cup last year, Neville played in all but one of their 13 Champions' League ties and never finished on the losing side. His success has rubbed off on England, too. He has tasted defeat in just four of his 34 international games since making his debut against Japan five years ago.

Typically, when he was suspended for the semi-finals of Euro 96, England lost to Germany on penalties. Neville was also missing when England suffered a 2-1 loss in Sweden and a 1-0 play-off defeat by Scotland — their only reverses along the qualifying road to Euro 2000.

He has tasted defeat in just four of his 34 international games.

Neville insists his natural position is at full-back, and his almost telepathic understanding down the right with David Beckham makes him England's obvious No 2.

Phil Neville

Mr Versatile

CLUB: Manchester United
PREVIOUS CLUBS: None
BIRTH DATE/PLACE: 21 January 1997, Bury
HEIGHT/WEIGHT: 5ft 10in/11st 11lb
ENGLAND DEBUT: 23 May 1996 v China
(Beijing, won 3-0)
ENGLAND APPEARANCES: 23 (0 goals)

'I have enjoyed so many great games with United and collected a number of winners' medals over the years. But that doesn't diminish my appetite to be part of a successful England squad.'

Don't mention England's left-sided problems to Phil Neville. The Manchester United defender is convinced they don't exist.

The younger of English football's most famous brothers simply cannot understand why Kevin Keegan has spent so much time trying to unearth another left-back when he has been fit and available all along.

True, he might be naturally right-footed. But that has never proved a hindrance in more than 150 games for his club. And though more than half his England caps have been won while filling in for his absent brother on the right, he has never struggled when allowed to start in his natural position on the other flank.

The European Championships are nothing new to him, though. He was a late call-up to Terry Venables' Euro 96 squad less than a month after making his England debut in China. His presence alongside Gary in that team made them England's first brothers since the Charltons, but Phil never got the chance to play in the Championship finals and was kept on the sidelines by the awesome presence of Stuart Pearce.

At club level, Phil has always followed in his brother's footsteps. He graduated from United's youth academy two years after Gary and was 18 months behind him breaking into the senior side. A talented schoolboy cricketer, he played for England at Under-14 and Under-15 levels and was invited to play cricket for Lancashire before deciding his future was in football.

Don't mention England's left-sided problems to Phil Neville. He is convinced they don't exist.

Michael Owen

Watch him go

CLUB: Liverpool
PREVIOUS CLUBS: None
BIRTH DATE/PLACE: 14 December 1979, Chester
HEIGHT/WEIGHT: 5ft 8in/11st
ENGLAND DEBUT: 11 February 1998 v Chile
(Wembley, lost 0-2)
ENGLAND APPEARANCES: 18 (5 goals)

'I have always been confident in my ability to partner Alan Shearer. We looked dangerous together in the World Cup and I know it can work again.'

A t the age of just 20, Michael Owen has already developed shoulders broad enough to carry the weight of a nation's expectations. Now let us hope his hamstrings can also bear the strain.

The form and fitness of the Liverpool striker have been England's obsession ever since the baby-faced youngster exploded onto the scene at the 1998 World Cup finals.

Everyone who had seen him in Anfield action knew he was something special. But nobody realised just how special.

Everyone who had seen him in Anfield action knew he was something special. But nobody realised just how special. Not since Pele's contribution to Brazil's 1958 triumph had a

31

teenager made such a dramatic impact on the World Cup. It wasn't just England supporters who were thrilled by Owen's efforts. Football lovers around the world were transfixed by the grace and control of a natural predator.

Owen was just 17 and a half when he made his first appearance for Liverpool, coming on as a substitute for Patrik Berger at Wimbledon. Robbie Fowler, watching from the stand, was totally unsurprised when the kid scored. 'He's going to be better than me,' he predicted.

The following season, the duo were launched as Liverpool's front-line strike partnership. Owen scored 23 goals, Fowler 13. Two months after his 18th birthday, he became England's youngest player this century when he was handed his senior international debut by Glenn Hoddle.

In May 1998 he became the youngest scorer in England history when he netted against Morocco in Casablanca, a feat he repeated less then a month later when England were heading for World Cup defeat by Romania in Toulouse. But it was Owen's magnificent solo goal in that memorable second round clash with Argentina which brought France 98 to life. It was also a goal which was to transform his life. He returned from France as the hottest property in the game — and a national pin-up.

He returned from France as the hottest property in the game — and a national pin-up.

But Owen's angelic looks also hide a steely determination and total fearlessness in the penalty box. Yet there is always a price to

pay for such an all-action style and Owen has been plagued by hamstring problems for the past year. The original injury, suffered against Leeds in April 1999, ruled him out of action for five months.

Then a recurrence of the injury at the start of this year suggested a more deep-rooted problem, much to the anxiety of Liverpool manager Gerard Houllier and England boss Kevin Keegan.

Ray Parlour

The grafter

CLUB: Arsenal
PREVIOUS CLUBS: None
BIRTH DATE/PLACE: 7 March 1973, Romford, Essex
HEIGHT/WEIGHT: 5ft 10in/11st 12lb
ENGLAND DEBUT: 27 March 1999 v Poland as substitute (Wembley, won 3-1)
ENGLAND APPEARANCES: 6 (0 goals)

'I thought I was on my way out when Arsene Wenger arrived at Arsenal. People were fed up with me not doing the business. But I proved them wrong.'

The most improved player at Highbury has already won two of the toughest battles of his career. Now he must convince Kevin Keegan that he can do a better job on the right than David Beckham.

Parlour readily admits that he was in real danger of chucking his promising career away a few years ago. Sidetracked by an undisciplined lifestyle, it was only when close friend Tony Adams faced up to his own personal problems that the penny suddenly dropped.

The arrival of Arsene Wenger seemed to signal the beginning of the end of Parlour's Arsenal career. But he knuckled down to business on the training ground, worked overtime on his control and won over Wenger with his open-minded attitude to change.

He has since blossomed into a top quality midfield performer. His speed and strength, allied to a newly-developed awareness which also allows him to play as stand-in right-back, makes him a key figure at Highbury.

No one contributed more to Arsenal's League and Cup double in 1998, a fact acknowledged by the club's supporters who voted him their Player of the Year.

Many observers reckon his form that year warranted a place in England's World Cup squad, but though he was included in the initial 30-man squad he failed to make the final cut. It wasn't until Kevin Keegan took charge that Parlour won his first cap, replacing Steve McManaman in the 3-1 win over Poland last March. His first starting role came against Luxembourg six months later.

Now he must convince Kevin Keegan that he can do a better job on the right than David Beckham.

Parlour's problem now is that he is in direct competition with David Beckham for the right midfield role at Euro 2000. The Manchester United star is almost certain to start against Portugal on 12 June. The Arsenal man is ready and willing to take over at a moment's notice.

Kevin Phillips

Hotshot from Hitchin

CLUB: Sunderland
PREVIOUS CLUBS: Baldock Town, Watford
(joined Sunderland in July 1997 for £375,000)
BIRTH DATE/PLACE: 25 July 1973, Hitchin, Herts
HEIGHT/WEIGHT: 5ft 7in/11st
ENGLAND DEBUT: 28 April 1999 v Hungary
(Budapest, 1-1)
ENGLAND APPEARANCES: 3 (0 goals)

'When Southampton rejected me at 18, I told them I would prove them wrong. I always believed in my ability.'

Sunderland's Kevin Phillips has soccer's most valued ability — he knows how to score goals ... and lots of them.

Rejected by a string of clubs as a schoolboy, the tiny teenager drifted into non-League football with Baldock Town and was working in a bakery until Watford spotted his potential. They paid just £10,000 for his services and were rewarded with a goal every other game.

Canny Sunderland boss Peter Reid was first to react to Phillips' growing reputation, paying £375,000 to take the striker to Wearside. Arriving at a club demoralised by recent relegation from the top flight, Phillips immediately set about revitalising the city with 35 goals in his first season.

Even though a toe injury kept him on the sidelines for almost four months at the start of the 1988-89 campaign, he still contributed an amazing 25 goals as

Sunderland stormed away with the First Division Championship. But it was only when Phillips was given a belated taste of Premiership football that people began to sit up and take notice. Twenty Premier League goals by the end of January left every other marksman trailing in his wake and confirmed his ability to score at any level.

It was only when Phillips was given a belated taste of Premiership football that people began to sit up and take notice.

Kevin Keegan had already awarded Phillips a shock first cap in Hungary in April 1999 when Michael Owen was ruled out by injury. His first international goal has yet to arrive. But it is only a matter of time.

Jamie Redknapp

Smooth operator

CLUB: Liverpool
PREVIOUS CLUBS: Bournemouth (joined Liverpool in January 1991 for £350,000)
BIRTH DATE/PLACE: 25 June 1973, Barton-on-Sea, Hants
HEIGHT/WEIGHT: 6ft/12st 10lb
ENGLAND DEBUT: 6 September 1995 v Colombia (Wembley, 0-0)
ENGLAND APPEARANCES: 17 (1 goal)

'My whole England career has been up and down because of the injuries I've suffered. I still feel I can show people more.'

Jamie Redknapp has been on the brink of international stardom for the past four years. Euro 2000 could finally provide his breakthrough.

The Liverpool ball player gave what Kevin Keegan described as his finest England performance in November's play-off victory in Scotland. Typically, within a week he was injured again.

That has been the all-too depressing pattern for Redknapp since making his international debut nearly five years ago. He was crocked for months after a brief but impressive display against Scotland at

Euro 96. Another whack from the South Africans the following year ruled him out of the England picture for a further 16 months.

Released from schoolboy terms by Spurs to sign for his dad at Bournemouth, he was quickly on the move again when, at the age of just 17, he became Kenny Dalglish's last signing for Liverpool. New boss Graeme Souness quickly recognised young Redknapp's potential and pitched him into Premiership action alongside fellow kids Robbie Fowler and Steve McManaman.

Terry Venables once identified David Beckham and Jamie Redknapp as the future of English football.

Terry Venables, who gave Redknapp his first England cap, once identified David Beckham and the Liverpool lad as the future of English football. Whether there is room for them in the same team remains open to doubt and they have started just three games together for their country. But if Keegan can come up with a formation to accommodate two such gifted talents, England will be the only winners.

David Seaman

Give him a big hand

CLUB: Arsenal
PREVIOUS CLUBS: Leeds, Peterborough, Birmingham, QPR (joined Arsenal in May 1990 for £1.3 million)
BIRTH DATE/PLACE: 19 September 1963, Rotherham
HEIGHT/WEIGHT: 6ft 4in/14st 10lb
ENGLAND DEBUT: 16 November 1988 v Saudi Arabia (Riyadh, 1-1)
ENGLAND APPEARANCES: 56

'We all know we didn't play well in the qualifiers. But now we're through to Euro 2000 and that is all that really matters. We've got to make the most of this opportunity.'

D avid Seaman has been written off more times than a stock car but, fitness permitting, the Arsenal ace will still be England's first choice keeper at Euro 2000.

A series of niggling injuries and a couple of uncharacteristic errors at the start of the season had convinced his critics that the man they call 'Safe Hands' was finally starting to feel his years. And with Nigel Martyn enjoying a new lease of life behind Leeds United's live-wire youngsters, it seemed to be only a matter of time before Seaman handed over his gloves.

Fortunately for England, it was a plot which Seaman had not read. For it was his stunning reflex save from Scotland's Christian Dailly which saved Kevin Keegan from a Wembley play-off disaster and allowed England to edge into Euro 2000 through the back door. So it was hardly surprising when Keegan confirmed that the Arsenal man only needed to steer clear of injuries to guarantee his place in England's opening game against Portugal on 12 June.

The England coach knows that

Seaman's experience will be invaluable when the heat is really on in Belgium and Holland. The 36-year-old goalkeeper is a veteran of two World Cup finals as well as Euro 96, when his famous penalty save from Scotland's Gary McAllister set England up for a run to the semi-finals.

Considering he is regarded as the world's outstanding keeper of the past decade by many observers, it seems remarkable that he has yet to win his 60th cap for England. In ten years at Highbury, he has won two League Championships, two FA Cups, the League and Cup and the European Cup-Winners' Cup. Yet it was only when Terry Venables became England coach in 1994 that

Seaman really established himself ahead of Martyn and Tim Flowers as his country's undisputed number one.

The England coach knows that Seaman's experience will be invaluable when the heat is really on in Belgium and Holland.

Now the laid-back Yorkshireman, once the world's most expensive goalkeeper who has turned out to be one of soccer's shrewdest signings, is under threat again. But the 'Rotherham Rock' won't be losing any sleep over it.

Paul Scholes
Diamond geezer

CLUB: Manchester United
PREVIOUS CLUBS: None
BIRTH DATE/PLACE: 16 November 1974, Salford
HEIGHT/WEIGHT: 5ft 8in/11st 10lb
ENGLAND DEBUT: 24 May 1997 v S. Africa as
    substitute (Old Trafford, won 2-1)
ENGLAND APPEARANCES: 21 (9 goals)

'Playing at Euro 2000 will be a fantastic experience for all of us. Hopefully, we will have a good chance of winning the competition.'

Sir Bobby Charlton describes him as 'a little diamond,' and 'a national treasure', and he will be one of the first names on Kevin Keegan's team sheet in Belgium and Holland.

Paul Scholes, the Salford assassin, will just keep his head down and do his very best to stay out of the spotlight. But don't mistake his modesty for indifference. For here is a young man who cares about his football with a fierce passion.

He was on target in his first start for his country, helping England to a morale-boosting win against Italy during Le Tournoi in 1997. He scored against Tunisia in England's opening game of France 98 and, of course, he notched a hat-trick in Keegan's first match in charge against Poland.

For Manchester United, his strike rate is even more impressive. The flame-headed 25-year-old never seems to score a meaningless goal. His 11-goal contribution to the famous treble of 1999 included Champions' League strikes against Barcelona, Bayern Munich, Brondby and Inter Milan as well as the FA Cup final clincher against Newcastle at Wembley. He had netted a further five times this season until his progress was briefly halted by a Christmas hernia operation that kept him out of United's World Club Championships campaign in Brazil.

Bobby Charlton describes him as 'a little diamond,' and 'a national treasure'.

Alan Shearer
The final shoot out

CLUB: Newcastle
PREVIOUS CLUBS: Southampton, Blackburn
(joined Newcastle in July 1996 for £15 million)
BIRTH DATE/PLACE: 13 August 1970, Newcastle
HEIGHT/WEIGHT: 6ft/12st 6lb
ENGLAND DEBUT: 19 February 1992 v France
(Wembley, won 2-0)
ENGLAND APPEARANCES: 57 (28 goals)

'Everyone knows what England means to me. When I am standing there listening to the National Anthem, it's such a great moment.'

Kevin Keegan bullishly insists that England can win Euro 2000 despite their unimpressive qualifying campaign. But he knows that won't happen unless Alan Shearer is on fire.

The good news for the England coach is that his battle hardened skipper is injury free and enjoying the sort of form which will terrorise every team at the championships. His performances for Newcastle in recent months have been reminiscent of the powerhouse striker who twice smashed the British transfer record and rewrote Premiership history. Bobby Robson's arrival at St James' Park, coupled with the emergence of Duncan Ferguson as a fit and functional strike partner, has given Shearer a new lease of life.

contribution to that success, he became the first player to score 100 Premiership goals and had netted 122 in 138 games for Blackburn by the time they sold him to Kevin Keegan's Newcastle for a world record £15 million.

Another serious injury, this time a broken shin and torn ankle ligaments, left Shearer's career in the balance again at the start of the 1997-98 season. Yet though it might have cost him a yard of pace, the poacher's instincts remain as keen as ever and he is now on the brink of 300 career goals.

Although it was Glenn Hoddle who first appointed Shearer to the England captaincy, Keegan's first act as international coach was to confirm that the country's top scorer would retain the skipper's armband. His act of faith was instantly rewarded as Shearer struck six goals in Keegan's first seven games in charge.

England supporters will be praying he gets those goals at Euro 2000. There will be no more welcome sight than Shearer reeling away in delight, his right arm raised in that oh-so-familiar celebration.

No defender has ever enjoyed an easy ride from Shearer. Strength of character and body, allied to boundless determination and an amazing will to win, makes him a fearsome opponent. And that is the way he has always been, ever since he became the youngest hat-trick scorer in First Division history when he dismantled Arsenal in only his fourth appearance for Southampton in 1988. He was still only 21 when he scored on his England debut against France and just a couple of months older when Blackburn made him the most expensive player in the country.

Strength of character and body, allied to boundless determination and an amazing will to win, makes him a fearsome opponent.

Even eight months on the sidelines following a serious cruciate ligament injury suffered on Boxing Day 1992 could not dent the lad's self-confidence. He returned stronger than ever to fire Blackburn to an unlikely League Championship triumph in 1994-95. Voted Footballer of the Year for his 34 goal-

Tim Sherwood

You're never too late

CLUB: Tottenham
PREVIOUS CLUBS: Watford, Norwich, Blackburn
(joined Spurs in February 1999 for £3.8 million)
BIRTH DATE/PLACE: 6 February 1969, St.Albans, Herts
HEIGHT/WEIGHT: 6ft/12st 9lb
ENGLAND DEBUT: 27 March 1999 v Poland
(Wembley, won 3-1)
ENGLAND APPEARANCES: 3 (0 goals)

'It took me a long, long time to win my first England cap. All I can do now is make the most of any further opportunities that might come my way.'

Not too many players make their international debut seven weeks after their 30th birthday, but having gatecrashed England's Euro 2000 party at an age when many players are considering retirement, Tim Sherwood is determined to go the distance.

The tough-tackling midfielder has enjoyed a career renaissance since signing for Spurs in a £3.8 million deal at the start of last year. He needed just a month in a Spurs shirt to convince Kevin Keegan that he was

the man to anchor England's midfield in the absence of David Batty.

Sherwood's most obvious quality is his ability to be first to the ball. He relishes a battle and is never afraid to put a foot in and rattle opponents with the strength of his challenges. Yet to dismiss him as nothing more than a midfield hard man would be doing him a great disservice. His tactical awareness and eye for an opening is matched only by his ability to deliver the ball at the right time.

He relishes a battle and is never afraid to put a foot in and rattle opponents with the strength of his challenges.

Kenny Dalglish knew just what Sherwood could offer when he made him one of his first signings for Blackburn in February 1992. The player certainly didn't disappoint, captaining Rovers to the League Championship in 1995. But that title medal remains the only reward he has to show for a 500-game career which has also taken in service at Watford and Norwich.

Gareth Southgate

He'll be spot on

CLUB: Aston Villa
PREVIOUS CLUBS: Crystal Palace (joined Villa in July 1995 for £2.5 million)
BIRTH DATE/PLACE: 3 September 1970, Watford
HEIGHT/WEIGHT: 6ft/12st 8lb
ENGLAND DEBUT: 12 December 1995 v Portugal as substitute (Wembley, 1-1)
ENGLAND APPEARANCES: 34 (1 goal)

> 'I will never be allowed to forget that penalty miss. But I wouldn't hesitate to put myself on the spot again if it was required.'

Gareth Southgate inadvertently took his place in football folklore when his Euro 96 spot-kick was saved by German keeper Andreas Kopke and

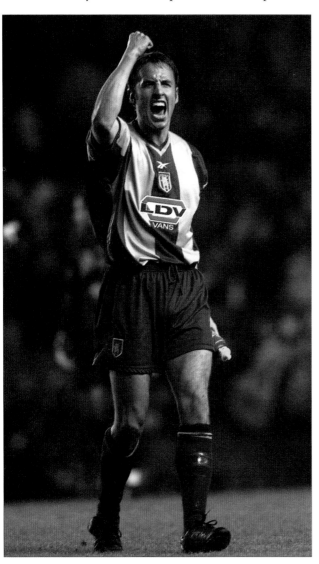

cost England their first appearance in a European Championship final.

At least he could console himself with the knowledge that he has more than proved himself for both club and country in the intervening years. And now he is heading for another European Championships determined to play his part in an England story with a happier ending.

Southgate had started just two games for his country when he was asked by Terry Venables to partner Tony Adams at the heart of England's Euro 96 defence. The quiet authority with which he set about the job impressed the entire country. Now he has more than 30 caps under his belt as well as the experience of the 1998 World Cup finals, even though he was mysteriously relegated to the bench after the opening 2-0 win against Tunisia.

In Gareth Southgate he [Keegan] has a man who can handle anything the tournament might throw at England.

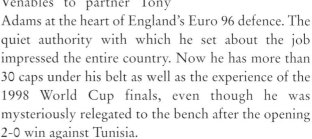

Watching Southgate in action, it is hard to believe that he spent the first six years of his career in midfield. It was only after his £2.5 million move from Crystal Palace to Villa that he was converted into the cultured, ball-playing central defender of today.

Kevin Keegan might have a number of defensive permutations open to him at Euro 2000. But in Gareth Southgate he has a man who can handle anything the tournament might throw at England.

Ian Walker

Gloving every minute

CLUB: Tottenham
PREVIOUS CLUBS: None
BIRTH DATE/PLACE: 31 October 1971, Watford
HEIGHT/WEIGHT: 6ft 2in/13st 1lb
ENGLAND DEBUT: 18 May 1996 v Hungary as substitute (Wembley, won 3-0)
ENGLAND APPEARANCES: 3

> 'I have been much happier with my form in the past year. I've been through a tough spell but now I am moving in the right direction again.'

It is now more than three years since the Spurs keeper Ian Walker won his last England cap and he knows he is unlikely to add to his meagre collection at Euro 2000. Yet at least he has the consolation of being back in the frame after edging his way ahead of Tim Flowers as Kevin Keegan's third choice goalie.

Walker had managed just 35 minutes of international action when he was included in Terry Venables' squad for Euro 96. That experience of participating in a major international event was to stand him in good stead. But his harshest lesson was to come eight months later, when he was handed his first start in a vital World Cup qualifier against Italy and cruelly blamed for Gianfranco Zola's deflected Wembley winner.

Worse was to follow for Walker. The arrival of Christian Gross as Spurs boss coincided with a dramatic dip in his club form, culminating in two long spells out of the first team and his last minute axeing from Glenn Hoddle's 1998 World Cup squad.

He was actually on the bench when George Graham succeeded the hapless Gross in October

With both Seaman and Martyn now into their mid-30s, Walker's time may yet still come.

1998, but it didn't take him long to win back his place. A run of just six goals conceded in 17 games culminated in Spurs winning last season's Worthington Cup Final and Walker's excellent form has continued throughout this season.

With both Seaman and Martyn now into their mid-30s, Walker's time may yet still come.

Late on the scene

Emile Heskey

Bruno can floor 'em

CLUB: Leicester City
PREVIOUS CLUBS: None
BIRTH DATE/PLACE: 11 January 1978, Leicester
HEIGHT/WEIGHT: 6ft 2in/13st 12lb
ENGLAND DEBUT: 28 April 1999 v Hungary as substitute (Budapest, 1-1)
ENGLAND APPEARANCES: 5 (0 goals)

The Leicester powerhouse battered his way into Kevin Keegan's plans when he scared the life out of Argentina's defence at Wembley in February.

Few observers had regarded Heskey as a serious contender for a place at Euro 2000 prior to that high-profile friendly inter-national. Although he had already won four caps for brief substitute appearances against Hungary, Bulgaria, Belgium and Scotland, it was widely believed that the raw striker was just making up the squad numbers in the absence of the injured Michael Owen and Robbie Fowler. But his efforts against the world-ranked Argentines forced Kevin Keegan into a major rethink. Although he was unable to come up with his first England goal, he did just about everything else against a defence rated among the meanest in the game.

> ### His efforts against the world-ranked Argentines forced Kevin Keegan into a major rethink.

Yet Heskey knows he still has work to do before he can take his squad place for granted. Leicester fans dubbed him 'Bruno' because of his resemblance to the former British heavyweight champion rather than the number of times he goes down. But rival supporters still claim that 'Lino' would be a more appropriate nickname given the amount of time he spends on the floor.

Liverpool boss Gerard Houllier, though, has no reservations about Heskey's ability and signed the player in a £11 million deal in March 2000. Leicester did all they could to keep their star man but were always fighting a losing battle.

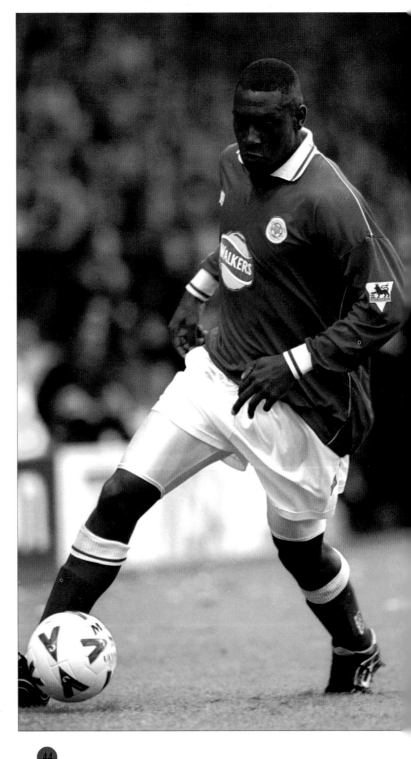

Jason Wilcox

Left foot forward

CLUB: Leeds
PREVIOUS CLUBS: Blackburn (signed by Leeds in December 1999 for £3 million)
BIRTH DATE/PLACE: 15 July 1971, Bolton
HEIGHT/WEIGHT: 6ft/11st
ENGLAND DEBUT: 18 May 1996 v Hungary (Wembley, won 3-0)
ENGLAND APPEARANCES: 3 (0 goals)

From First Division reserve to Euro 2000 contender in the space of six months, Jason Wilcox is enjoying a remarkable international renaissance which could yet provide the solution to England's problem left-sided position.

He could yet provide the solution to England's problem left-sided position.

At the start of this season, Wilcox feared his career was on the slippery slope to oblivion following relegation from the Premiership with Blackburn. Fortunately for the Bolton-born wide-man, Leeds boss David O'Leary had not forgotten about him. Wilcox might not have been considered good enough for Rovers' first division scraps, but O'Leary knew that his experience could prove invaluable to his young team's title challenge. Within two months of his arrival at Elland Road, Wilcox was the shock addition to Keegan's squad for the Argentina game.

Even when acting manager Howard Wilkinson handed him a shock call-up against France last year, there was little to suggest that Wilcox was about to become an England regular. But Keegan, nudged by O'Leary's foresight, realised that here was a player with the ability to provide the service down the left which had been his greatest headache in his first year as manager. Wilcox provided more accurate crosses in one match against Argentina than his predecessors had managed in their previous half dozen. Euro 2000 suddenly beckons.

Dennis Wise

Little big man

CLUB: Chelsea
PREVIOUS CLUBS: Wimbledon (joined Chelsea in May 1990 for £1.6 million)
BIRTH DATE/PLACE: 16 December 1966, Kensington
HEIGHT/WEIGHT: 5ft 6in/ 10st 11lb
ENGLAND DEBUT: 1 May 1991 v Turkey (Izmir, won 1-0)
ENGLAND APPEARANCES: 14 (1 goal)

Nobody needs to tell Dennis Wise that he would have won 50 caps by now were it not for his suspect temperament. The volatile Chelsea skipper knows all too well that he is own worst enemy. But at 33 years old, it is a bit too late to start trying to change his ways.

Controversy and Wise have gone hand in hand ever since the day he walked out of a trial with Southampton as a headstrong kid after they refused to pay his travelling expenses from London. He has been in hot water virtually every season since, clocking up enough disciplinary points to keep a small FA committee in full-time employment.

Glenn Hoddle, Wise's former manager at Chelsea, wouldn't touch the player with a bargepole during his two-year spell as England boss and even the call from Kevin Keegan earlier this year was overshadowed by Wise's latest misconduct charge for a tunnel bust-up against Wimbledon.

Yet for all his faults, there is no denying that the Stamford Bridge captain is a hugely influential player. His 14 international appearances might have been spread over nine years, yet Wise has made a significant contribution in each of those games.

Of course he is a fearless ball-winner and ferocious competitor.

Of course he is a fearless ball-winner and ferocious competitor, but his detractors often overlook the accuracy and perception of Wise's passes and his ability to spot a forward run into the channels.

The little fella is a winner. And we haven't got too many of those right now.

Richard Wright

One for the future

CLUB: Ipswich
PREVIOUS CLUBS: None
BIRTH DATE/PLACE: 5 November 1977, Ipswich
HEIGHT/WEIGHT: 6ft 1in/14st 5lb
ENGLAND DEBUT: –
ENGLAND APPEARANCES: 0

Ipswich's giant young goal-keeper almost certainly won't play at Euro 2000, but there's a fair chance he could go to the finals for the experience.

The way things stand at present, it is a straight choice between Wright and Tottenham's Ian Walker for the third keeper's spot in Keegan's final squad. Wright might be short on international appearances but is generally regarded as the finest young goalie in the country. Walker, at 28, might be the safer choice right now. But Keegan has one eye on the future and is thought to favour giving Wright the trip.

The Ipswich rookie already knows a thing or two about being thrown in at the deep end.

The Ipswich rookie already knows a thing or two about being thrown in at the deep end. He was only 17 when he made his senior debut for a club that had already been relegated from the Premier League and leaking goals at an alarming rate. The three games he managed at the end of that disastrous 1994-95 season remain the only Premiership matches in Wright's CV, yet he has proved himself at every other level, including England schoolboy, youth and Under-21.

ENGLAND V GERMANY – IT'S ALWAYS THE GERMANS

by Steven Howard, Chief Soccer Writer, *The Sun*

Beethoven, Mercedes Benz, Dortmunder Union lager, Claudia Schiffer — four of the greatest products ever to emerge from Germany. And then there's football.

Three-time winners of the World Cup and three-time European Champions, Deutchland have been 'uber alles' for far longer than we care to remember. And yet we just can't resist, can we?

In a game England had to win, [Sir Alf] sent out an England midfield with all the finesse of a building site demolition ball.

'66 HEROES... That famous World Cup triumph remains England's only major trophy.

As comedian Frank Skinner remarked when glued to the box during the 1994 World Cup in the USA: 'I was watching Germany and I got up to make a cup of tea. I bumped into the telly and Klinsmann fell over....' Then there was Stan Boardman, who once famously observed: 'Jeermans? I've never forgiven them for bombing our nan's chippie.' And on it goes.

Well, if you can't beat 'em, you might as well slaughter 'em. As we prepare to take the road to Charleroi, where England meet Germany on 17 June, we have to reflect on the following sobering statistic. Since beating our Anglo-Saxon cousins at Wembley in 1966, we have faced them six times in tournament competition and won, er, well, we haven't actually won any!

Even Wales overcame the old Bosch 1-0 in Cardiff in a 1991 European Championship qualifier. And Northern Ireland, that other fearsome football power, managed back-to-back 1-0 Euro qualifier wins in the early Eighties. Since Nobby's dance under the Twin Towers 34 years ago, we have met our nemesis on 14 occasions and managed just two wins — 2-0 at Wembley in 1975 and 3-0 in Mexico City 10 years later.

Mind you, there were always the two 'moral' victories when we were shamelessly beaten on penalties at both the 1990 World Cup and the 1996 European Championships. Before that last one, Terry Venables was asked what he most admired about Germany. The astute England coach replied: 'Their results.'

That World Cup final triumph aside, we have not had much to crow about when it comes to matters Germanic since England strung together a now astonishing seven straight wins between 1935 and 1966 itself. Included in this run was the Stanley Matthews-inspired silencing of 110,000 Berliners in 1938 as England handed out a 6-3 humbling to Hitler's sporting representatives.

Now the diplomatic service has always prided itself on its *sange froid* but surely blood has never flowed quite so coolly through veins as it did through Sir Nevile Henderson's that day. On an afternoon that was supposed to reflect the unstoppable might of the Third Reich, the British ambassador leaned over to Air Marshall Goering, offered him his binoculars and said: 'What wonderful goals. You really ought to taker a closer look.' Goering, no doubt, determined there and then to take a closer and more personalised look at Sir

Nevile once the tedious business of crossing the Channel had been accomplished.

Anglo-German footballing relations had all started one Christmas Day during the earlier fracas with that 100-a-side kick-about on a muddy stretch of No Man's Land.

Tommy v Jerry gave way to Bobby Moore against Franz Beckenbauer at Wembley 50 years later and Beckenbauer is still at it to this day as he wrestles with Bobby Charlton — another old 1966 adversary — for the right to stage the 2006 World Cup.

I don't know who won that initial Inter-Trench Cup but I'm sure the esteemed football correspondent of the *Illustrated London News* made full reference to the Germans' well-organised 40-man defence and the diving attributes of the centre-forward in the pointy helmet.

But it was another centre-forward — the most famous in German history — who was to exact full revenge for defeat at Wembley in 1966, four years later in Mexico. Gerd Muller was his name, 'Der Bomber' his sobriquet, goals his speciality. He scored a record 365 in the Bundesliga, 68 in 62 internationals, the winning goal in the 1974 World Cup Final — and the killer third in Mexico against England in 1970. Much has been made down the years of goalkeeper Peter

HAT-TRICK KING...Geoff Hurst's trio eventually saw off the Germans at Wembley in 1966.

CROWNING GLORY...A proud Bobby Moore with the Jules Rimet trophy.

Bonetti's part in England's downfall but surely Alf Ramsey must shoulder some of the blame for bringing off both Bobby Charlton and Martin Peters with England leading 2-1?

Two years on and it was the Germans again as England were ejected from the European Championships — beaten 3-1 at Wembley and then held 0-0 in Berlin. The Germans had a team that purred along like the top range models that eased their way off the production-line at the Bavarian Motor Works.

From Maier in goal to Grabowski on the wing, the side was an exceptional collection of talent with players like Beckenbauer, Breitner, Hoeness, Netzer and Muller. After England's trouncing at Wembley,

TEMPER, TEMPER... Pulses rise during Euro 96.

German boss Helmut Schoen said: 'I'm sure my friend Sir Alf will have many ideas for the return game.' Sadly, Sir Alf's mind was blank. In a game England had to win, he sent out an England midfield with all the finesse of a building-site demolition ball.

Even now I wince at the memory of some of the tackles from Norman Hunter and Peter Storey, who rampaged round the Olympic Stadium like warthogs in a mudbath. The graceful Netzer, kicked from pillar to post, said afterwards: 'I have Storey's autograph — from my ankle to my knee.' Schoen added: 'Some of England's tackling was brutal and aimed at the bone.' And Sir Alf? 'The referee didn't please me at all,' he said. 'He was petty and even penalised good tackles.'

It was this match, I believe, that firmly planted in the English mind the image of the Germans as a load of namby-pamby, boy-scout, play-actors who didn't like it up 'em. Debatable though it was at the time, it was an image that gained credence over the next 20 years and still persists to this day.

Yet, strangely enough, the next time the two countries met, England played the Germans at their own sophisticated game and won 2-0 at Wembley. Alan Hudson starred on his debut, played one more game and was then consigned to the international backwaters. Thus have England always treated their

ANGUISH... A toe-nail's width denies Gazza Euro glory.

few rare talents. At the time, they had maverick riches in abundance in Hudson himself, Peter Osgood, Charlie George, Rodney Marsh and Stan Bowles. Bowles, of course, was of whom Orient manager George Petchey said before a cup tie: 'The trouble with Stan is that he falls over as soon as anyone sneezes — and a lot of my players have colds.'

England and Germany would not meet in serious action again until the second phase of the 1982 World Cup in Spain. They drew 0-0 — a result that eventually led to England's elimination — with the old animosity still very much alive. Skipper Bryan Robson said of left-back Paul Breitner, an arch critic of English football: 'I've never met a team which squeal quite like the Germans — especially Breitner. I put my hand out to hold him off and he went down screaming as if I'd dropped him one.'

Three years later, a momentous occasion took place in Mexico City where England thumped their big rivals 3-0 with Kerry Dixon scoring twice on his first start for England. Needless to say he would start only another four games for his country.

It was an extraordinary affair with Glenn Hoddle, believe it or not, actually winning praise for his ... tackling. On closer inspection, it was not quite the miracle it would appear as the Germans had only arrived the day before the game and, as such, were not exactly jack-booting about at a height 7,500 feet above sea level.

Now we enter the more modern Gazza era and those penalty shoot-out dramas in Turin in 1990 and at Wembley in 1996. The performance in Italy was the best against Germany in a top tournament since 1966. We could and, perhaps, should have won but for Chris Waddle hitting the woodwork at 1-1. Then Waddle and Stuart Pearce blazed wide — brave England the losers, clever Pizza Hut the winners.

> ### Andreas Moller, an example of infuriating Teutonic arrogance at its worst, converted the winner. We all wanted to drop him one.

Six years on and it was Gareth Southgate in the queue for the quattro formaggio and extra pepperoni as the German penalty-taking machine ground on remorselessly. Andreas Moller, an example of infuriating Teutonic arrogance at its worst, converted the winner. We all wanted to drop him one.

And so to today or, rather, Charleroi in June. Once again we are getting ourselves into a lather, writing off the Germans as not just ageing European champions but almost decrepit. Mein Gott!, they were even beaten twice by the USA last year. True enough, they are on the slide with five defeats in 18 games since being pummelled 3-0 by Croatia at France 98.

And no more Sammer, Moller, Hassler, Basler or Klinsie. Then again, they always come up with something — just as they did at Euro 96 when they still managed to emerge triumphant despite playing the final with half a side missing. This time they will still be able to call on AC Milan striker Oliver Bierhoff, Liverpool-bound Markus Babbel and the Bayern

SICKENER...Waddle blazes wide and the Germans celebrate.

Munich quartet of goalkeeper Oliver Kahn, Jens Jeremies, Carsten Jancker and Lothar Matthaus.

Yes, Matthaeus, a man seemingly born with those famous Heidelberg duelling scars, now 39 and approaching his 150th game for his country. He made his debut as long ago as 1980, has played in a joint record five World Cups and a record 25 World Cup games. A beaten finalist in 1986, he finally reached the pinnacle in 1990 when he skippered Germany to victory over Argentina. He was European Footballer of the Year and World Soccer Player of the Year that same year. But injury kept him out of the 1992 European Championships before, amazingly, he was recalled for international duty at France 98. Last season he was taken off during the European Cup Final against Manchester United with 10 minutes to go and Bayern cruising to a 1-0 win.

Little more than 10 minutes later, there were people on the pitch, United had won and it was all over. He is not the only member of the Bayern team who will be looking for victory over England this summer as revenge for that unbelievable night in Barcelona.

So here we go again. England v Germany. Get your tin hats on. And if that's not enough, there's always the 2002 World Cup qualifiers...

England v Germany	
Total Games	22
Wins for England	9
Wins for Germany	8
Drawn	5
Goals for England	38
Goals against England	29

Germany

Group A

HOW THEY GOT THERE

TURKEY 1 GERMANY 0 (10 OCTOBER 1998)	GERMANY 6 MOLDOVA 1 (4 JUNE 1999)
MOLDOVA 1 GERMANY 3 (14 OCTOBER 1998)	FINLAND 1 GERMANY 2 (4 SEPTEMBER 1999)
N. IRELAND 0 GERMANY 3 (27 MARCH 1999)	GERMANY 4 N. IRELAND 0 (8 SEPTEMBER 1999)
GERMANY 2 FINLAND 0 (31 MARCH 1999)	GERMANY 0 TURKEY 0 (9 OCTOBER 1999)

EUROPEAN CHAMPIONSHIP RECORD

With three Championship triumphs and two further appearances in the final, Germany have an unrivalled European record of success.

And when you consider that they didn't even enter the first two tournaments, it is clear that here is a team which can never be written off as major contenders.

It was in 1972 that Germany first made their mark on the Championships, beating host nation Belgium 2-1 in the semi-finals and then the USSR 5-3 in the final in Brussels. Gerd Muller, probably the greatest in a long

THE COACH
Erich Ribbeck

Handed the thankless task of overhauling an ageing German side after the disappointment of the 1998 World Cup, when they went out in the quarter-finals to Croatia. Ribbeck, who will celebrate his 63rd birthday during the finals, is now in his 33rd year as a coach. After an unimpressive playing career with Wuppertaler and Viktoria Cologne, he moved into management with Rot-Weiss Essen in 1967. A studious tactician with a reputation for discipline, he soon became one of the most respected coaches in Germany and has seen service with Eintracht Frankfurt, Kaiserslautern, Borussia Dortmund, Bayer Leverkusen, SV Hamburg and Bayern Munich. Also spent six years on the German coaching staff between 1978 and 1984, helping the national team win the 1980 European Championships and reach the 1982 World Cup final.

line of German goal scoring machines, scored twice in both games.

Four years later it was Muller's namesake, Dieter, whose goals powered them through to the final in Yugoslavia, but this time they lost 5-3 on penalties to Czechoslovakia after a 2-2 draw.

Normal service was resumed four years later in Italy, when Horst Hrubesch netted both goals as the Germans beat Belgium 2-1 in the final at Rome's Olympic Stadium.

Yet German confidence was surprisingly dented during the 1984 Championships in France, when defeat by Spain cost them first round qualification.

And although they had the striking prowess of Jurgen Klinsmann and Rudi Voller on their own patch four years later, it wasn't enough to prevent a semi-final defeat by the Dutch.

In 1992 it was the turn of rank outsiders Denmark to provide the shock of the tournament when they beat the highly-rated Germans 2-0 in the Stockholm final.

But the Germans can never be written off and just when it appeared that they were finally on the wane, Berti Vogts' team stormed back to win Euro 96, first beating England on penalties in one of the most dramatic semi-finals in history and then accounting for the Czech Republic with Oliver Bierhoff's golden goal.

STAR PLAYERS

▼ Oliver Kahn
AGE: 30. CLUB: BAYERN MUNICH

● Firmly established as Germany's first choice keeper after taking over from the veteran Andreas Kopke shortly after Euro 96.

● Started with home-town club Karlsruher, he became the most expensive goalkeeper in his country's history when he joined Bayern Munich for £2 million six years ago.

● Suffered a cruciate knee injury which ruled him out for six months shortly after joining Bayern but has since helped them win the UEFA Cup and reach last year's Champions' League final.

▶ Oliver Bierhoff
AGE: 32. CLUB: AC MILAN (ITALY)

● Late developing striker who is now regarded as one of the deadliest marksmen in Europe despite his advancing years.

● Failed to make an impact during his early years in Germany, when he played for five different clubs including SV Hamburg and Borussia Moenchengladbach.

● It wasn't until he moved to Austria Salzburg and then Ascoli in Italy that he started to make a name for himself. Won his first German cap at 27, scored the Euro 96 winner and earned a dream move to Milan.

▶ Christian Ziege
AGE: 28. CLUB: MIDDLESBROUGH (ENGLAND)

● Attacking left-sided wing-back who actually started his career in goal and was hailed as 'the new Andreas Brehme' by former German boss Berti Vogts.

● Made his international debut seven years ago after representing Germany at every level, including the Olympic team.

● Left Bayern Munich for AC Milan after Euro 96 and signed for Middlesbrough in a £4 million deal last summer.

Portugal
Group A

HOW THEY GOT THERE

HUNGARY 1 PORTUGAL 3 (6 SEPTEMBER 1998)
PORTUGAL 0 ROMANIA 1 (10 OCTOBER 1998)
SLOVAKIA 0 PORTUGAL 3 (14 OCTOBER 1998)
PORTUGAL 7 AZERBAIJAN 0 (26 MARCH 1999)
LIECHTENSTEIN 0 PORTUGAL 5 (31 MARCH 1999)
PORTUGAL 1 SLOVAKIA 0 (5 JUNE 1999)
PORTUGAL 8 LIECHTENSTEIN 0 (9 JUNE 1999)
AZERBAIJAN 1 PORTUGAL 1 (4 SEPTEMBER 1999)
ROMANIA 1 PORTUGAL 1 (8 SEPTEMBER 1999)
PORTUGAL 3 HUNGARY 0 (9 OCTOBER 1999)

EUROPEAN CHAMPIONSHIP RECORD

Considering the brilliance of the Portuguese team of the 1960s, it is amazing to think that Portugal did not qualify for the European Championship finals until 1984. Their semi-final clash with France that year in Marseille was one of the greatest games in Championship history, eventually losing 3-2 to the brilliance of Michel Platini.

Another 12 years passed before Portugal got another shot at glory at Euro 96. They came to life with a 3-0 thrashing of the fancied Croats. But once again they could not sustain that intensity and were bundled out by the Czech Republic in the quarter-finals.

THE COACH
Humberto Coelho
Twice Portuguese footballer of the year and one of his country's most capped players, 50-year-old Coelho was appointed national coach in succession to Antonio Oliveira in December 1997. The former Benfica defender won eight Portuguese championships during a 19-year playing career. Moved into coaching with Salgueiros in 1985 and a year later joined Sporting Bragas, where he remained until taking over as national boss in 1997.

STAR PLAYERS

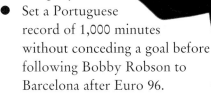

▶ ## Vitor Baia
AGE: 30. CLUB: PORTO
- Brilliant goalkeeper who only went for trial with Porto to keep a friend company.
- Set a Portuguese record of 1,000 minutes without conceding a goal before following Bobby Robson to Barcelona after Euro 96.
- Loaned back to Porto at start of the season, Baia has been instrumental in the club's progress in the Champions' League.

◀ ## Luis Figo
AGE: 27. CLUB: BARCELONA (SPAIN)
- Quick and dangerous wide man.
- Won the World Youth Cup in 1991 and the Portuguese Cup with Sporting Lisbon three years later.
- He is regarded as one of Spanish football's most successful imports.

▶ ## Paolo Sousa
AGE: 29. CLUB: INTER MILAN (ITALY)
- Midfield creator who came to prominence when he helped Portugal win the 1989 World Youth Championships.
- Quit Benfica for Sporting Lisbon following a wage dispute in 1994.
- Moved to Juventus in 1995, winning Italian League and Cup double.

Romania

Group A

HOW THEY GOT THERE

ROMANIA 7 LIECHTENSTEIN 0 (2 SEPTEMBER 1998)	ROMANIA 2 HUNGARY 0 (5 JUNE 1999)
PORTUGAL 0 ROMANIA 1 (10 OCTOBER 1998)	ROMANIA 4 AZERBAIJAN 0 (9 JUNE 1999)
HUNGARY 1 ROMANIA 1 (14 OCTOBER 1998)	SLOVAKIA 1 ROMANIA 5 (4 SEPTEMBER 1999)
ROMANIA 0 SLOVAKIA 0 (27 MARCH 1999)	ROMANIA 1 PORTUGAL 1 (8 SEPTEMBER 1999)
AZERBAIJAN 0 ROMANIA 1 (31 MARCH 1999)	LIECHTENSTEIN 0 ROMANIA 3 (9 OCTOBER 1999)

EUROPEAN CHAMPIONSHIP RECORD

Considering that Romania are one of the few nations to have entered every European Championship since the competition's inception, their record is pretty dismal. In 11 attempts, this is the only the third time they have qualified for the final stages, and they have yet to win a game. Romania first reached the finals in 1984. But, after drawing 1-1 with Spain, they lost to both West Germany and Portugal and were on their way home again.

Two further unsuccessful qualifying campaigns followed until they reached the 1996 finals in England. Once again they flattered to deceive, losing all their first round games to France, Bulgaria and Spain.

THE COACH
Emerich Jenei

Back for his second spell as national coach following the shock sacking of Victor Piturca two weeks after Romania's unbeaten qualifying campaign for Euro 2000. Piturca was axed for arguing with his star players and 63-year-old Jenei has been left to pick up the pieces. During his first spell as Romanian coach, Jenei led the team to the 1990 World Cup finals in Italy.

STAR PLAYERS

▸ **Dan Petrescu**
AGE: 32. CLUB: CHELSEA (ENGLAND)

● Attacking wing-back now in his 12th year as a full international.
● Voted one of the outstanding players of the 1994 World Cup in the USA.
● After further spells with Genoa and Sheffield Wednesday, he signed for Chelsea in November 1995 for £2.3 million.

◂ **Gheorge Hagi**
AGE: 35. CLUB: GALATASARAY (TURKEY)

● International debut at the age of 18.
● The outspoken Romanian captain enjoyed spells with Real Madrid and Barcelona before moving to Turkey.
● Recently named Best Romanian footballer of the 20th century.

▸ **Gica Popescu**
AGE: 32. CLUB: GALATASARAY (TURKEY)

● Experienced sweeper and central defensive organiser.
● Like most Romanian internationals, he started at Steaua before his first move abroad to PSV Eindhoven.
● Spent one ill-fated year in England with Spurs before a £3.2 million move to Barcelona in 1995. Now in Turkey with brother-in-law Hagi.

Italy Group B

HOW THEY GOT THERE

WALES 0 ITALY 2 (5 SEPTEMBER 1998)   ITALY 4 WALES 0 (5 JUNE 1999)
ITALY 2 SWITZERLAND 0 (10 OCTOBER 1998)   SWITZERLAND 0 ITALY 0 (9 JUNE 1999)
DENMARK 1 ITALY 2 (27 MARCH 1999)   ITALY 2 DENMARK 3 (8 SEPTEMBER 1999)
ITALY 1 BELARUS 1 (31 MARCH 1999)   BELARUS 0 ITALY 0 (9 OCTOBER 1999)

EUROPEAN CHAMPIONSHIP RECORD

Considering Italy's complete obsession with football, their record in the European Championships is distinctly underwhelming. Although they did win the title on the first occasion they qualified for the finals in 1968, there was a distinct element of luck about that triumph in their own back yard.

After all, it was only the toss of a coin which put them through to the final after a goalless draw with the USSR in Rome. And they needed a replay in the Olympic Stadium to see off the challenge of Yugoslavia, winning 2-0 with goals from Riva and Anastasi after a 1-1 draw.

It wasn't until Italy hosted the tournament again in 1980 that they next reached the finals, and again they were hampered by their negative approach.

Marco Tardelli's single goal against England, coupled with goalless draws against Spain and Belgium, put them through to the third place final. But they paid the price for another draw against the Czechs when they lost 9-8 on penalties.

Things looked brighter in Germany in 1988 when the Italians drew with the hosts then beat Spain and Denmark to progress to the semi-finals. But once again they flattered to deceive, losing 2-0 to the USSR.

And if Zoff is to survive his Championship ordeal, he will surely have taken note of Italy's shock exit at Euro 96. After comfortably beating Russia in their opening game, coach Arrigo Saachi decided to rest most of his key players for their next match against the Czech Republic. The arrogance of his decision was to rebound on Saachi as the Czechs won 2-1.

Although Italy were back to full strength for a 0-0 draw with Germany, it was not enough to take them through to the next round. Exit Saachi.

THE COACH
Dino Zoff

No coach will be under greater pressure at Euro 2000 than the man who captained Italy to World Cup glory in 1982. Less than two years after taking over from Cesare Maldini, the knives are already out for Zoff. A dismal run of results, including home defeats by Denmark and Belgium, meant Italy failed to get a seeding for Euro 2000 or the World Cup qualifiers. Nobody appeared better suited to the job than 58-year-old Zoff, who was a goalkeeping legend during his years with Napoli and Juventus. As well as the 1982 World Cup, he was also a member of Italy's European Championship winning side of 1968 and won seven Championships, two Italian Cups and the UEFA Cup with Juve. But his coaching style has proved distinctly less successful.

STAR PLAYERS

▶ **Alessandro del Piero**
AGE: 25. CLUB: JUVENTUS

- Brilliant striker forcing his way back into the international reckoning after being ruled out for nine months by a serious knee injury.
- The 'Golden Boy' of Italian football, he forced his way into the Under-21 team while still a teenager at lower division Padova.
- Moved to Juve in 1993 and voted Italy's Young Player of the Year two years later. Has won two Series A championships and played three times in the European Cup final.

▼ **Paolo Maldini**
AGE: 31. CLUB: AC MILAN

- Still undisputed Italian captain despite his father, Cesare, resigning as national coach in 1998.
- Unflappable left-sided defender who is rated the outstanding Italian player of his generation and arguably the best full-back in the world.
- Voted world player of the year in 1994, he has played more than 100 times for Italy since making his debut against Yugoslavia in 1988.

▶ **Gianluigi Buffon**
AGE: 22. CLUB: PARMA

- Agile young goalkeeper who has more than justified Zoff's faith in him since replacing the established Angelo Peruzzi and Gianluca Pagliuca in the Italian team a year ago.
- Helped Parma win the Italian Championship at the age of 20 and was a key figure in last year's UEFA Cup triumph.
- Conceded just two goals in six qualifying games and extraordinary late save in final game against Belarus spared Italy the ignominy of the play-offs.

Belgium
Group B

STAR PLAYERS

▶ **Luc Nilis**
AGE: 32. CLUB: PSV EINDHOVEN (HOLLAND)

● Most experienced player in the Belgian squad.
● He fell out with former coach Leekens but had a change of heart in December following the appointment of Waseige.
● Voted Dutch footballer of the Year in 1996 and is half of Europe's most prolific strike partnership with Ruud Van Nistelrooy.

◀ **Gilles de Bilde**
AGE: 28. CLUB: SHEFFIELD WEDNESDAY (ENGLAND)
● The former bad boy of Belgium, he is now back in favour.
● Once kicked out of Belgian football when he was prosecuted for breaking an opponent's jaw and cheek.
● Restored his battered reputation in Holland with PSV Eindhoven before a £3 million transfer to England last July.

HOW THEY GOT THERE
QUALIFIED AUTOMATICALLY AS JOINT HOSTS.

EUROPEAN CHAMPIONSHIP RECORD

This will be Belgium's first championship finals appearance for 16 years and life will certainly be much tougher than when they last hosted the event. That was back in 1972, when they qualified for the four-team finals for the first time but were beaten 2-1 by the West Germans in the semi-finals.

Eight years later and they exceeded all expectations when they reached the final at Euro 80. Sadly, they were unable to maintain their form in the red-hot atmosphere of the Olympic Stadium, and went down 2-1 to Germany.

It was to be a different story four years later in France, where an opening 2-0 win against Yugoslavia was followed by a 5-0 mauling from France. A 3-2 defeat by Denmark confirmed their first round exit.

THE COACH
Robert Waseige
A shock choice to replace the unpopular George Leekens last August, Waseige has orchestrated an unexpected revival to raise spirits in the Belgian camp. The avuncular 60-year-old might have been voted Belgian coach of the Year in 1986, 1994 and 1995, yet in 28 years of club management he had managed only one major trophy. But form has been much improved for the Belgian squad since his arrival.

▶ **Marc Wilmots**
AGE: 31. CLUB: SCHALKE 04 (GERMANY)

● Powerful attacking midfielder nicknamed 'The Wild Boar' because of his rampaging style.
● Made his name as a teenage striker with Mechelen, but later moved into midfield.
● He scored the winning penalty when Schalke 04 beat Inter Milan in the 1997 UEFA Cup final.

Sweden
Group B

HOW THEY GOT THERE

SWEDEN 2 ENGLAND 1 (5 SEPTEMBER 1998) ENGLAND 0 SWEDEN 0 (5 JUNE 1999)
BULGARIA 0 SWEDEN 1 (14 OCTOBER 1998) SWEDEN 1 BULGARIA 0 (4 SEPTEMBER 1999)
SWEDEN 2 LUXEMBOURG 0 (27 MARCH 1999) LUXEMBOURG 0 SWEDEN 1 (8 SEPTEMBER 1999)
POLAND 0 SWEDEN 1 (31 MARCH 1999) SWEDEN 2 POLAND 0 (9 OCTOBER 1999)

EUROPEAN CHAMPIONSHIP RECORD

Incredibly, this is the first time Sweden have ever qualified for the finals in the competition's 40-year history. The only time they have made an appearance was when they hosted the tournament in 1992.

Yet even with home advantage they could not shake off their negative attitude during the opening phase of games, drawing 1-1 with France and edging past neighbours Denmark.

It was only when facing elimination in their final group game against England that they finally threw caution to the wind and Brolin's late winner was enough to take them through to the quarter-finals.

Germany, though, were to prove a tougher proposition in Stockholm. Despite goals from Brolin and Kennet Andersson, Germany always had the upper hand and went through 3-2.

THE COACH
Tommy Soderberg

Handed the thankless task of succeeding the hugely popular Tommy Svensson, Soderberg has won few fans despite his team's impressive form. He immediately set about instilling greater discipline into the team and his influence is reflected in the fact that they conceded just one goal en route to Euro 2000. But they scored just ten goals in eight games, and they now face an attacking dilemma.

STAR PLAYERS

▼ Magnus Hedman
AGE: 27. CLUB: COVENTRY (ENGLAND)
- Unflappable goalkeeper rated one of the best in English football.
- Replaced Swedish legend Thomas Revelli after failure to qualify for the 1998 World Cup finals.
- Married to Swedish pop star Magdalena.

▶ Stefan Schwarz
AGE: 31. CLUB: SUNDERLAND (ENGLAND)
- Voted Sweden's Player of the Year in 1999.
- A key figure in Sweden's run to the last four at the 1994 World Cup.
- Unable to settle in English football during an unhappy spell at Arsenal, he is now back in the Premiership.

◀ Fredrik Ljungberg
AGE: 23. CLUB: ARSENAL (ENGLAND)
- Goalscoring midfield man.
- Moved from Halmstads to Arsenal for £3 million in September 1998.
- He is known as 'Sid' at Highbury because he looks like late punk star Sid Vicious.

Turkey

Group B

HOW THEY GOT THERE

TURKEY 3 N. IRELAND 0 (5 SEPTEMBER 1998)	MOLDOVA 1 TURKEY 1 (8 SEPTEMBER 1999)
TURKEY 1 GERMANY 0 (10 OCTOBER 1998)	GERMANY 0 TURKEY 0 (9 OCTOBER 1999)
TURKEY 1 FINLAND 3 (14 OCTOBER 1998)	
TURKEY 2 MOLDOVA 0 (27 MARCH 1999)	**PLAY-OFFS**
FINLAND 2 TURKEY 4 (5 JUNE 1999)	REP. OF IRELAND 1 TURKEY 1 (13 NOVEMBER 1999)
N. IRELAND 0 TURKEY 3 (4 SEPTEMBER 1999)	TURKEY 0 REP. OF IRELAND 0 (17 NOVEMBER 1999)

EUROPEAN CHAMPIONSHIP RECORD

Despite the backing of the most vociferous travelling supporters at Euro 96 in England, Turkey were totally overwhelmed by the occasion. They lost all three group games without scoring a goal.

But coach Mustafa Denizli points to his team's qualifying record, when they beat and drew with the Germans, as an indicator that they are much better prepared this time.

Turkey, whose only other experience of a major competition was at the 1954 World Cup, insist that qualifying for the finals is not enough this time. Yet the fact that the players have already received a Range Rover and $200,000 bonus already suggests they are not expecting to be around for the later stages.

THE COACH

Mustafa Denizli

A hero in Turkey after their play-off victory over the Irish in November, yet Denizli's future as national coach remains in the balance. Denizli, 50, was appointed successor to Fatith Terim in October 1996. A former left-winger with Altay, he spent eight years at Galatasaray as coach and then technical director.

STAR PLAYERS

▶ **Umit Davala**
AGE 26. CLUB: GALATASARAY

● Has played in every position bar goalkeeper for Galatasaray.
● Singled out as his club's most important player by Fatith Terim, the former Turkish coach.
● Scored memorable goal against Juventus in last year's Champions' League.

◀ **Sergen Yalcin**
AGE 27. CLUB: FENERBAHCE

● Turkey's midfield creator who is just as famous for his playboy lifestyle.
● Won three Turkish Championships with Besiktas before moving to Istanbulpor.
● Famed for his love of racing — he owns a string of horses — and Istanbul's nightclubs.

▶ **Hakan Sukur**
AGE: 28. CLUB: GALATASARAY

● The best-known player in Turkish football.
● Moved to Italy for £3 million in 1995.
● Lasted just five months in Torino before returning, homesick, to Galatasaray.

Norway

Group C

HOW THEY GOT THERE

NORWAY 1 LATVIA 3 (6 SEPTEMBER 1998)	NORWAY 1 GEORGIA 0 (30 MAY 1999)
SLOVENIA 1 NORWAY 2 (10 OCTOBER 1998)	ALBANIA 1 NORWAY 2 (5 JUNE 1999)
NORWAY 2 ALBANIA 2 (14 OCTOBER 1998)	NORWAY 1 GREECE 0 (4 SEPTEMBER 1999)
GREECE 0 NORWAY 2 (27 MARCH 1999)	NORWAY 4 SLOVENIA 0 (8 SEPTEMBER 1999)
GEORGIA 1 NORWAY 4 (28 APRIL 1999)	LATVIA 1 NORWAY 2 (9 OCTOBER 1999)

EUROPEAN CHAMPIONSHIP RECORD

Norway's European Championship pedigree may not be much to shout about — they've never qualified for the finals before. Yet that doesn't mean they will be heading for their opening match in Rotterdam with any sort of inferiority complex.

Their self-belief is based on their shock defeat of Brazil during the 1998 World Cup, when two goals in the last seven minutes from Tore Andre Flo and Kjetil Rekdal were enough to take them through to the second round.

And with a squad chock-full of stars from the English Premiership, Norway are convinced their functional, no frills style will claim a few more scalps at Euro 2000.

THE COACH
Nils Johan Semb

Semb admits his first few months in charge of the team were 'a bit of a nightmare'. After seven years as Egil Olsen's right-hand man, it was no shock when the studious Semb was promoted to the top job. But defeat by Latvia in his opening game — Norway's first home loss in seven years — and a scrappy draw in Albania had Norwegian fans demanding Olsen's return. Semb, 41, stuck by Olsen's controversial long-ball style and the players who had served his predecessors so well. And it eventually paid dividends. An unbeaten run of 15 games, including nine straight victories, swept Norway through to Euro 2000.

STAR PLAYERS

▶ **Tore Andre Flo**
AGE: 26. CLUB: CHELSEA (ENGLAND)

- Beanpole striker who has already scored more than 20 times for his country.
- Chelsea paid £300,000 to buy up the remaining few months of his Brann Bergen contract in May 1997.
- The subject of unsuccessful £15 million bids from Italy, he has kept the likes of Zola, Sutton and Weah on the sidelines at Chelsea.

◀ **Oyvind Leonhardsen**
AGE: 29. CLUB: TOTTENHAM (ENGLAND)

- Strong-running midfielder whose stamina is legendary in Norway.
- He joined Wimbledon for a mere £650,000 from Rosenborg Trondheim at the start of 1995.
- Lost his way following £4 million move to Liverpool, he has enjoyed a real revival in the past 12 months at Spurs.

▶ **Ole Gunnar Solskjaer**
AGE: 27. CLUB: MANCHESTER UNITED (ENGLAND)

- Lethal striker dubbed 'the baby-faced assassin'.
- Cost £1.5 million when he moved from Molde to Old Trafford four years ago.
- Scored the winning goal in the dying seconds of the European Cup final against Bayern Munich in Barcelona.

Spain Group C

HOW THEY GOT THERE

CYPRUS 3 SPAIN 2 (5 SEPTEMBER 1998)   SPAIN 9 SAN MARINO 0 (5 JUNE 1999)
ISRAEL 1 SPAIN 2 (14 OCTOBER 1998)   AUSTRIA 1 SPAIN 3 (4 SEPTEMBER 1999)
SPAIN 9 AUSTRIA 0 (27 MARCH 1999)   SPAIN 8 CYPRUS 0 (8 SEPTEMBER 1999)
SAN MARINO 0 SPAIN 6 (31 MARCH 1999) SPAIN 3 ISRAEL 0 (10 OCTOBER 1999)

EUROPEAN CHAMPIONSHIP RECORD

Spanish coach, Jose Antonio Camacho might be flavour of the month in Spain right now, but he is not under any illusions about the size of the task ahead at Euro 2000.

No team has a greater ability to shoot itself in the foot than the Spaniards and Camacho knows only too well that big-match bottle will be every bit as decisive as ability as the tournament unfolds.

He claims: 'The truth is we have no record to defend. Until we've won a major event we can't be compared with world champion sides or regarded as favourites for this.'

In fact, Spain have won the Championships once, but that was way back in 1964, when they beat the USSR 2-1 in the final at Madrid's Bernabeu stadium. Spain, swept along on a tide of nationalist fervour and inspired by the return of former European Footballer of the Year, Luis Suarez from Inter Milan, proved to

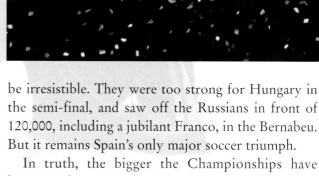

be irresistible. They were too strong for Hungary in the semi-final, and saw off the Russians in front of 120,000, including a jubilant Franco, in the Bernabeu. But it remains Spain's only major soccer triumph.

In truth, the bigger the Championships have become, the greater Spain's ability to self-destruct when the pressure is on.

True, they did reach the final again in 1984 when the championships were staged in France. Yet they got there by drawing three of their four games and beating Denmark on penalties in the semis before losing 2-0 to the irresistible French side in the final.

Since then it has been a familiar tale of promising much but achieving little, culminating at Euro 96 when they dominated their quarter-final clash with England but refused to throw caution to the wind and were beaten on penalties.

THE COACH
Jose Antonio Camacho

Camacho has taken less than two years to transform Spain into the most attractive team in Europe. He was only given the job in September 1998 after it had been rejected by the veteran Luis Aragones. He had just quit Real Madrid after just 22 days in charge. Yet despite his unimpressive coaching record at Rayo Vallocano, Seville and Espanol, Camacho has thrown off the ultra-cautious approach of his predecessor Javier Clemente. After a disastrous 3-2 defeat in his predecessor's last game in charge in Cyprus, Camacho's team then rattled in an amazing 40 goals in their next seven qualifiers.

STAR PLAYERS

▶ Luis Enrique
AGE: 29. CLUB: BARCELONA

- Fast breaking midfielder who sets up so many chances for Spain's forwards.
- Italian hard man Mauro Tassotti was handed a nine-match ban by FIFA when TV cameras captured him breaking Enrique's nose with an elbow during the 1994 World Cup.
- Rejected by Barcelona as a youth player, he controversially made his way to the Nou Camp from bitter rivals Real Madrid after Euro 96.

▲ Raul
AGE: 22. CLUB: REAL MADRID

- The golden boy of Spanish football and widely regarded as his country's most talented player since Emilio Butragueno.
- Lightning-quick striker, he broke into the Real Madrid team at the age of just 17 and has lived up to all expectations. Became the first Spaniard to finish top scorer in the Primera Division for seven years.
- The quietly-spoken charmer scored ten goals for Spain last year, including seven in the space of four amazing days against Austria and San Marino.

▶ Fernando Morientes
AGE: 24. CLUB: REAL MADRID

- Reliable, if unspectacular, striker whose partnership with close friend Raul will be crucial to Spanish hopes at Euro 2000.
- Suffered a dismal spell at Real under Dutch coach Guus Hiddink and hardly got a game for six months. Restored to the side by John Toshack, he responded with 15 goals in as many games.
- That form earned him a recall to the Spanish team and has maintained a goal a game record for his country.

Slovenia
Group C

HOW THEY GOT THERE

GREECE 2 SLOVENIA 2 (6 SEPTEMBER 1998)
SLOVENIA 1 NORWAY 2 (10 OCTOBER 1998)
SLOVENIA 1 LATVIA 0 (14 OCTOBER 1998)
GEORGIA 1 SLOVENIA 1 (27 MARCH 1998)
LATVIA 1 SLOVENIA 2 (5 JUNE 1999)
ALBANIA 0 SLOVENIA 1 (9 JUNE 1999)
SLOVENIA 2 ALBANIA 0 (18 AUGUST 1999)

SLOVENIA 2 GEORGIA 1 (4 SEPTEMBER 1999)
NORWAY 4 SLOVENIA 0 (8 SEPTEMBER 1999)
SLOVENIA 0 GREECE 3 (9 OCTOBER 1999)

PLAY-OFFS

SLOVENIA 2 UKRAINE 1 (13 NOVEMBER 1999)
UKRAINE 1 SLOVENIA 1 (17 NOVEMBER 1999)

EUROPEAN CHAMPIONSHIP RECORD

Considering that Slovenia only gained independence from Yugoslavia in 1991, it is hardly surprising that they have never qualified for any major championships before.

Yet they defied all the odds to finish runners-up to Norway in Group Two then refused to be overawed by the supposedly superior Ukranians in the play-offs last November.

Yet coach Srecko Katanec rejects claims that his team will be out of their depth in Holland and Belgium. 'We're not going to the finals to be cannon fodder,' he says.

THE COACH
Srecko Katanec
Slovenia's outstanding player of the past decade, 36-year-old Katanec won 31 caps as a hard-working midfield man for Yugoslavia during a seven-year international career. He only hung up his boots five years ago and had managed just half a season in club coaching with HIT Gorica before Slovenia put him in charge of their Euro 2000 campaign two years ago.

STAR PLAYERS

▶ **Zlatko Zahovic**
AGE: 29. CLUB: OLYMPIAKOS PIRAEUS (GREECE)

- Overwhelming choice as Slovenia's player of the year.
- Packed his bags for Red Star Belgrade at the age of 16 before moving to Porto.
- Scored seven goals in six European Champions' League games for Porto before a surprise move to Greece last summer.

▼ **Miran Pavlin**
AGE: 28. CLUB: KARLSRUHER (GERMANY)

- Midfield man who played a crucial role in the vital equaliser in the second-leg of their play-off triumph in the Ukraine.

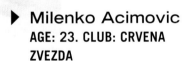

- Has spent the last five years of his career in Germany, first with Freiburg and now with Karlsruher.
- Summed up the mood of the Slovenian camp when he said: 'I am told the bookmakers are offering 80-1 against us winning Euro 2000. Bet on Slovenia and you will make a lot of money.'

▶ **Milenko Acimovic**
AGE: 23. CLUB: CRVENA ZVEZDA

- Slovenia's 'super-sub' who became a national hero when he scored the late winning goal in the play-offs against Ukraine.
- Midfield man who joined Red Star Belgrade from Olimpia Ljubljana in December 1997 before returning to Slovenia last summer.
- Acimovic claims: 'No one at Euro 2000 will know anything about us, but we are hungry for success.'

Yugoslavia
Group C

HOW THEY GOT THERE

YUGOSLAVIA 1 REP. OF IRELAND 0 (18 NOVEMBER 1998)	REP. OF IRELAND 2 YUGOSLAVIA 1 (1 SEPTEMBER 1999)
MALTA 0 YUGOSLAVIA 3 (10 FEBRUARY 1999)	YUGOSLAVIA 3 MACEDONIA 1 (5 SEPTEMBER 1999)
YUGOSLAVIA 4 MALTA 1 (8 JUNE 1999)	MACEDONIA 2 YUGOSLAVIA 4 (18 SEPTEMBER 1999)
YUGOSLAVIA 0 CROATIA 0 (18 AUGUST 1999)	CROATIA 2 YUGOSLAVIA 2 (9 OCTOBER 1999)

EUROPEAN CHAMPIONSHIP RECORD

Having been booted out of the 1992 finals because of United Nations sanctions against Serbia, Yugoslavia didn't even bother entering the tournament last time out.

Incredibly, they have twice finished runners-up despite the fact that they have only won two of their ten matches in the finals. The first, a pulsating 5-4 victory against the French, was enough to take them through to the 1960 final which they lost to the USSR. Eight years later they beat England 1-0 in the semis then lost a replayed final to Italy following a 1-1 draw.

Since then their record has been anything but impressive, with successive defeats by West Germany, Holland, Belgium, Denmark and France.

THE COACH
Vujadin Boskov

At 68-years-old, Boskov will be by far the most experienced coach at Euro 2000. With NATO's bombing campaign of Yugoslavia already underway, he could not have arrived for his second spell as national coach under more difficult circumstances. Yet in spite of being forced to cram their final five qualifiers into a hectic seven-week schedule, Boskov's boys still won through in the tightest of all the groups. Boskov, who won 57 caps as a player for Yugoslavia, has now been coaching across Europe for 35 years. He has worked in Holland, Spain, Italy and Switzerland as well as his home country, tasting success at Feyenoord, Real Madrid, Sampdoria, Roma and Napoli.

STAR PLAYERS

▶ **Predrag Mijatovic**
AGE: 31 CLUB: FIORENTINA (ITALY)
- Yugoslavia's chief striking hope at Euro 2000.
- Scored the goal that gave Real Madrid a record seventh European Cup triumph in 1998.
- Coach Boskov says: 'Mijatovic is such a great player, one of the best in Europe.'

◀ **Sinisa Mihajlovic**
AGE: 31. CLUB: LAZIO (ITALY)
- Solid defender and Yugoslavia's likely captain at Euro 2000.
- He has scored more free-kicks than any other player in Serie A history.
- He was part of the Lazio team which beat Real Mallorca in last year's Cup-Winners' Cup final.

▶ **Dejan Stankovic**
AGE: 21. CLUB: LAZIO (ITALY)
- Rising young star of Yugoslav football, he became the youngest player in Red Star Belgrade's history when he made his debut at 16.
- Mother and father both played professionally in Yugoslavia. Midfielder Stankovic won his first Yugoslav cap at just 19 and scored twice on his debut against South Korea.

- Won League and Cup double with Red Star before joining Lazio two years ago. He played in all eight of Yugoslavia's Euro 2000 qualifiers and scored the vital equaliser in their final game against Croatia.

Czech Republic Group D

HOW THEY GOT THERE

FAROE ISLES 0 CZECH REP. 1 (6 SEPTEMBER 1998)
BOSNIA-HERZEGOVINA 1 CZECH REP. 3
(10 OCTOBER 1998)
CZECH REP. 4 ESTONIA 1 (14 OCTOBER 1998)
CZECH REP. 2 LITHUANIA 0 (27 MARCH 1999)
SCOTLAND 1 CZECH REP. 2 (31 MARCH 1999)

ESTONIA 0 CZECH REP. 2 (5 JUNE 1999)
CZECH REP. 3 SCOTLAND 2 (9 JUNE 1999)
LITHUANIA 0 CZECH REP. 4 (4 SEPTEMBER)
CZECH REP. 3 BOSNIA-HERZEGOVINA 0
(8 SEPTEMBER 1999)
CZECH REP. 2 FAROE ISLES 0 (9 OCTOBER 1999)

THE COACH
Josef Chovanec

Appointed in January 1998 after the Czech's surprise failure to qualify for that year's World Cup finals, Chovanec has made a perfect start to his career as national coach, with a one hundred per cent record in their qualifying campaign. Chovanec, 40, won 52 caps for his country as a dominating sweeper during the 1980s and 1990s. He also won eight Czech championships at Sparta Prague. His attacking outlook as Sparta coach won him the nod from the Czech FA when they ousted Dusan Uhrin at the end of 1997. Regarded as 'one of the lads' by his players, he will have no shortage of support at Euro 2000.

EUROPEAN CHAMPIONSHIP RECORD

Czech Republic have qualified for Euro 2000 in style, by winning every game and compiling a maximum 30 points. But it's not just the form book which suggests that the Czech Republic will triumph in Holland and Belgium. History is also on their side.

No Czech team at the European Championship finals has ever finished lower than third place. With a perfect qualifying record this time and second place in FIFA's world rankings, few Czechs will settle for anything less than final glory.

They first made their mark on the competition in 1960, when they finished third after losing to the USSR and then beating France. But there was to be no stopping them in 1976, when they beat the Dutch 3-1 then held their nerve when the Germans scrambled a late equaliser to win the final in a famous penalty shoot-out. When it came to it, the Czechs held their nerve while the German's wilted. When Uli Hoeness blasted Germany's fourth kick over the bar, Antonin Panenka scored the winning penalty with an outrageous chip.

Four years later they made it through to the third place play-off, where they beat Italy, again on penalties. But it was in England, at Euro 96, that they came closest to emulating their 1976 triumph. Victories over Italy and Russia, saw them emerge from the so-called 'Group of Death'. In the quarter-finals they beat the unpredictable Portuguese 1-0 with a goal from Karel Poborsky and edged past the French on penalties in a tight semi-final.

That set-up a final showdown with the Germans but, sadly for the Czechs, they couldn't hold on to Patrik Berger's 59th minute goal and became the first nation to lose a major final to a golden goal.

STAR PLAYERS

▼ Karel Poborsky
AGE: 28. CLUB: BENFICA (PORTUGAL)

● Flying winger nicknamed 'The Express Train' due to his incredible pace.

● Snapped up by Manchester United for £3.75 million after Euro 96, his arrival coincided with the emergence of David Beckham and he was never able to hold down a regular place at Old Trafford.

● Offloaded to Benfica for £2 million in December 1997, a protracted deal which required UEFA intervention to get the money out of the Portuguese club.

▲ Patrik Berger
AGE: 26. CLUB: LIVERPOOL (ENGLAND)

● Goalscoring playmaker who has emerged as a key figure in Gerard Houllier's Liverpool revival.

● Arrived at Anfield in £3.25 million move from Borussia Dortmund after his goal in the Euro 96 final against Germany. He started his career with Slavia Prague.

● Banned from the Czech's first two Euro 2000 games against Holland and France after being red carded in meaningless last qualifier versus the Faroe Isles.

▼ Vladimir Smicer
AGE: 26. CLUB: LIVERPOOL (ENGLAND)

● Like many Czech stars, he cashed in on his country's fine performances at Euro 96 to earn move from Slavia Prague to Lens.

● His goals helped Lens capture the 1998 French Championship and, with a recommendation from Berger, he was transferred to Liverpool for £3.75 million last summer.

● Speedy forward who survived a serious knee injury suffered as a youngster in Prague.

France

Group D

HOW THEY GOT THERE

ICELAND 1 FRANCE 1 (5 SEPTEMBER 1998)   FRANCE 2 RUSSIA 3 (5 JUNE 1999)
RUSSIA 2 FRANCE 3 (10 OCTOBER 1998)   ANDORRA 0 FRANCE 1 (9 JUNE 1999)
FRANCE 2 ANDORRA 0 (14 OCTOBER 1998)   UKRAINE 0 FRANCE 0 (4 SEPTEMBER 1999)
FRANCE 0 UKRAINE 0 (27 MARCH 1999)   ARMENIA 2 FRANCE 3 (8 SEPTEMBER 1999)
FRANCE 2 ARMENIA 0 (31 MARCH 1999)   FRANCE 3 ICELAND 2 (9 OCTOBER 1999)

EUROPEAN CHAMPIONSHIP RECORD

Few nations can boast a better recent record than the French, who will be appearing at their fifth Championship finals at Euro 2000. Yet their initial efforts to be crowned Europe's best were a dismal failure, despite hosting the inaugural tournament in Paris, when only four teams qualified for the finals. A 5-4 semi-final defeat by Yugoslavia followed by a 2-0 defeat by the Czechs left France rock bottom in front of their own supporters. But worse was to follow as they failed to qualify for the next five championships.

It wasn't until they hosted the tournament again in 1984 that France finally came to life, and with the magnificent Michel Platini running the show, they were to prove irresistible. Platini scored an incredible nine goals as the French swept aside Denmark, Belgium, Yugoslavia and Portugal. They crowned a

THE COACH

Roger Lemerre

Euro 2000 will be Lemerre's first major championships as coach, but nobody doubts his ability to handle the pressure after acting as number two to Aime Jacquet during France's sensational World Cup triumph two years ago. Lemerre, 58, was three times voted French Footballer of the Year during a 24-year playing career with Sedan-Ardennes, Nantes, Nancy and Lens which stretched from 1961 to 1985. He immediately moved into coaching, graduating from Red Star to Strasburg via Lens and Paris Racing. He joined the French FA's technical centre in 1986, was appointed Aime Jacquet's assistant in 1997 and promoted to the top job in 1998.

magnificent achievement by beating an under-par Spanish team 2-0 in the final at the Parc des Princes. Predictably, the peerless Platini struck first, to bring his total to nine for the tournament, and a last-minute goal from Bruno Bellone wrapped things up.

Yet four years later they failed to qualify for the finals again and in 1992 were eliminated in the first round after failing to win any of their group games against Sweden, England and Denmark. By Euro 96, however, the French were clearly developing into a force to be reckoned with and fancied their chances of going all the way until beaten on penalties in the semi-finals by the Czech Republic.

Two years later and that promise was realised when they became world champions in front of their own fans, comprehensively beating the mighty Brazil in the final. It was their second victory in a major tournament on home soil in 14 years. Now the French will go into Euro 2000 convinced there is no better team in the world.

STAR PLAYERS

▶ **Marcel Desailly**

AGE: 31   CLUB: CHELSEA (ENGLAND)

- Powerhouse central defender who was the cornerstone of France's World Cup triumph.
- Won the European Cup with Marseille in 1993 and again with AC Milan the following year.
- Won two Italian Championships at Milan, now in his second season in English football following a £4.6 million move to Chelsea in June 1998.

▲ **Zinedine Zidane**

AGE: 27   CLUB: JUVENTUS (ITALY)

- Brilliant midfield playmaker who has been a regular in the French national side since 1994.
- Voted world player of the year in 1998, he capped a good World Cup that year with the first two goals in the final against Brazil.
- Joined Juventus after Euro 96 following spells with Cannes and Marseille.

▼ **Nicolas Anelka**

AGE: 21   CLUB: REAL MADRID (SPAIN)

- Controversial but gifted goalscorer who will bear France's attacking expectations in Belgium and Holland.
- Walked out of Paris St. Germain as a 17-year-old to sign for Arsenal's French manager Arsene Wenger.
- Won the League and FA Cup double in 1998 with Arsenal before a bitterly conducted £23 million transfer to Real Madrid last summer.

Holland
Group D

HOW THEY GOT THERE
QUALIFIED AS JOINT HOSTS WITH BELGIUM

demolishing any defence in the world. Despite losing their opening game to the USSR, there was to be no holding the Dutch that year in Germany. A Marco Van Basten hat-trick demolished England in Dusseldorf, and a 1-0 victory over the Republic of Ireland was enough to take them through to the last four.

Goals from Ronald Koeman and Van Basten accounted for bitter rivals Germany in the semi-final before the USSR were swept aside in the final by Gullit and a memorable angled volley from Van Basten.

Having finally landed their first major trophy, the Dutch looked set to repeat their triumph at Euro 92 but lost on penalties in the semi-finals to eventual winners Denmark after beating Scotland, Germany and drawing with the CIS.

And it was the same old story at Euro 96, where they were widely tipped to clinch the title. Those hopes were dashed when they were battered 4-1 by England during the group stage. Patrick Kluivert's consolation goal ensured they scraped through to the later stages, but the reprieve was short-lived. They lost on penalties again in the second round, this time to France.

EUROPEAN CHAMPIONSHIP RECORD

The nearly men of world football will start Euro 2000 as firm favourites in front of their own supporters, despite a disturbing run of 11 games without a win beginning in 1998. However, Holland's past record in this competition is no guide as to what to expect from the men in orange, who remain as unpredictable as they are talented.

It was not until 1976 that the Dutch first qualified for the Championship finals, losing their semi-final 3-1 to Czechoslovakia before beating Yugoslavia in the third-place play-off. That was the team containing such legends as Cruyff, Neeskens and Krol, yet four years later they fared little better when they went out in the first round in a group also containing Greece, West Germany and Czechoslovakia.

With Holland failing to qualify for the 1984 finals, it was left to a new generation of superstars to finally bring glory to the Netherlands. Enter Gullit, Van Basten and Rijkaard, an attacking force capable of

THE COACH
Frank Rijkaard
One of the finest midfielders in Dutch history, Rijkaard is now trying to emulate his playing success in his first coaching job. Appointed to succeed Guus Hiddink after the 1998 World Cup finals, Rijkaard is still unsure how his team will perform in competitive circumstances. But nobody knows more about Holland's amazing tendency to self destruct and he is determined to stamp out the indiscipline and rows which have blighted previous major tournaments. As a player with Ajax and AC Milan, 37-year-old Rijkaard won just about every top honour going, including three European Cup winners' medals. Alongside Ruud Gullit and Marco Van Basten, he was also instrumental in Holland's European Championship triumph in 1988.

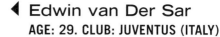

STAR PLAYERS

◀ Edwin van Der Sar
AGE: 29. CLUB: JUVENTUS (ITALY)

- Now first choice Dutch keeper after taking over from Chelsea's Ed De Goey, he is widely regarded as the best shot-stopper in Europe.
- Began his career with home town club Voorhout, moved to Noordwijk for a brief spell before joining Ajax, where he won four Dutch championships and the European Cup in 1995.
- An international for the past five years, he rejected a move to Manchester United to sign for Juventus on a 'Bosman' transfer last summer.

◀ Dennis Bergkamp
AGE: 30. CLUB: ARSENAL (ENGLAND)

- A teenage sensation, he replaced Marco Van Basten in the Ajax team at the age of 17 and was still a student when he played in the 1987 Cup-Winners' Cup Final.
- Voted Dutch Footballer of the Year in 1991 and 1992 before an unsuccessful move to Inter Milan in 1993 in a joint £8 million transfer with Wim Jonk.
- Left Italy for Arsenal in 1995 in a £7.5 million deal, and was voted England's Footballer of the Year in 1998 after helping the Gunners win the League and FA Cup double.

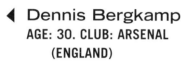

▲ Jaap Stam
AGE: 27. CLUB: MANCHESTER UNITED (ENGLAND)

- The powerful centre-half played for Zwolle, Cambuur and Willem II before joining PSV Eindhoven at the end of 1995 and forced his way into the Dutch side soon after Euro 96.
- Became the most expensive defender in the world when he joined United from PSV Eindhoven for £10.75 million in May 1998.
- Won the Champions Cup, the League Championship and the FA Cup in his first season in English football.

Denmark

Group D

HOW THEY GOT THERE

BELARUS 0 DENMARK 0 (5 SEPTEMBER 1998)	DENMARK 2 SWITZERLAND 1 (4 SEPTEMBER 1999)
DENMARK 1 WALES 2 (10 OCTOBER 1998)	ITALY 2 DENMARK 3 (8 SEPTEMBER 1999)
SWITZERLAND 1 DENMARK 1 (14 OCTOBER 1998)	
DENMARK 1 ITALY 2 (27 MARCH 1999)	**PLAY-OFFS**
DENMARK 1 BELARUS 0 (5 JUNE 1999)	ISRAEL 0 DENMARK 5 (13 NOVEMBER 1999)
WALES 0 DENMARK 2 (9 JUNE 1999)	DENMARK 3 ISRAEL 0 (17 NOVEMBER 1999)

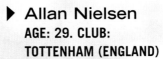

▶ **Allan Nielsen**
AGE: 29. CLUB: TOTTENHAM (ENGLAND)

- Midfield ball winner who remains central to Johansson's plans despite being unable to hold down a regular first team place at Spurs.
- A schoolboy genius who was signed by Bayern Munich when only 17, he managed just one game in three years for the Germans before being sent back to Denmark.
- Scored within 30 seconds of his Danish debut against Armenia in 1995.

EUROPEAN CHAMPIONSHIP RECORD

Denmark will always be known as football's ultimate party people after their sensational Stockholm triumph at Euro 92, actually winning the tournament after having been drafted in as last-minute replacements for Yugoslavia.

They weren't able to successfully defend their title four years later, going out in the first round.

Yet the Danes have a Euro record which stands comparison with much bigger soccer nations. They finished fourth in 1964 and only lost on penalties to Spain in the 1984 semi-finals.

But they also suffered the ignominy of losing all three games at Euro 88, and with Holland, France and the Czech Republic waiting round the corner this time, a similar fate cannot be ruled out.

◀ **Jon Dahl Tomasson**
AGE: 23. CLUB: FEYENOORD (HOLLAND)

- Powerful young striker now piecing his career back together in Holland after a nightmare year with Newcastle.
- Signed by Kenny Dalglish from Heerenveen for £2.5 million, he scored just three goals before being flogged to Feyenoord.
- Scored six goals in Denmark's final five qualifying games for Euro 2000.

▼ **Peter Schmeichel**
AGE: 36. CLUB: SPORTING LISBON (PORTUGAL)

- Danish legend with close on 120 caps for his country.
- Manchester United signed him from Brondby in 1991.
- Captained United to Champions' League glory in his final game for the club before moving to Portugal last summer.

THE COACH

Bo Johansson

Denmark's Swedish-born coach has achieved a near miracle getting his team through to the Euros after a disastrous start to their qualifying campaign. They failed to win any of their first four games, but everything suddenly fell into place last summer, culminating in a famous victory in Italy. Israel proved little obstacle in the play-offs and now 57-year-old Johansson shrugs off the mountain facing Denmark in Euro 2000's 'Group of Death'.

Doing it the hard way
Group 5

SWEDES IN CHARGE

A desperate start for England and their under-pressure coach Glenn Hoddle. Despite getting off to a flier through Alan Shearer's second minute free-kick, they fail to capitalise on their advantage and fall to pieces after conceding two scrappy goals in three minutes. First Andreas Andersson's shot goes in with the aid of deflections off Tony Adams and David Seaman. Twelve minutes from half-time, Gareth Southgate's attempted clearance hits Paul Scholes and Johan Mjallby heads in. To compound England's misery, Paul Ince is red carded by Italian ref Pierluigi Collina for a wild challenge on Henrik Larsson. He swears at the ref and throws v-signs at the Swedish fans and the England bench before being dragged away and is subsequently hit with a three-match ban.

Sweden 2 (A. Andersson, Mjalby)   **England 1** (Shearer)

5 September 1998, Solna
SWEDEN: Hedman, Nilsson, P.Andersson, Bjorklund, Kamark (Lucic 82), Schwarz, A.Andersson (D Andersson 89), Mjallby, Ljungberg, Larsson, Pettersson.
ENGLAND: Seaman, Anderton (Lee 42), Le Saux, Southgate, Adams, Campbell (Merson 74), Redknapp, Ince, Shearer, Owen, Scholes (Sheringham 86).

I SALUTE YOU... Shearer's strike couldn't prevent defeat in Solna.

England 0   Bulgaria 0

10 October 1998, Wembley
ENGLAND: Seaman, Anderton (Batty 67), Hinchcliffe (Le Saux 34), G.Neville, Southgate, Campbell, Lee, Scholes (Sheringham 77), Shearer, Owen, Redknapp.
BULGARIA: Zdrakov, Yordanov, Zagorcic, Kirilov, Kishishev, Iliev (Gruev 63), Yankov, M.Petkov, Naidenov, Stoichkov (Bachev 60), Hristov (Ivanov 90).

Another dismal effort from England and suddenly Euro 2000 qualification is starting to look distinctly dodgy. Robbed of his first choice midfield by injuries and suspension, Hoddle's stand-in playmakers fail to deliver against a Bulgarian side without most of their best players and still reeling from a recent 3-0 home defeat by Poland. The visitors' blanket defence is rarely stretched by England, who manage just one shot on target all match. One of England's worst Wembley performances in living memory.

DISMAL... Another poor finish, this time by Owen, sums up a shoddy performance against Bulgaria.

ON TARGET...Owen's opener set up a 3-0 win in Luxembourg.

A win at last, but it's still not enough to halt the cascade of criticism pouring down on Hoddle. Hardly surprisingly, England are a bundle of nerves again and only avert disaster when Luxembourg's Danny Theis blasts a sixth-minute penalty over the bar. Michael Owen steadies the ship with a 19th minute goal but an Alan Shearer penalty and a last-minute strike from Gareth Southgate do little to placate angry England fans expecting a goal feast. Hoddle is booed off the pitch by travelling supporters. It is to prove his last competitive match as England coach.

Luxembourg 0   England 3
(Owen, Shearer pen, Southgate)

14 October 1998, Luxembourg City
LUXEMBOURG: Koch, Ferron, L.Deville, Funck, F.Deville (Alverdi 84), Theis (Holtz 61), Saibene, Strasser, Posing, Cardoni, Christophe (Amodio 78).
ENGLAND: Seaman, Anderton (Lee 63), P.Neville, Southgate, Ferdinand, Campbell, Beckham, Batty, Shearer, Owen, Scholes (Wright 76).

Paul Scholes heralds the start of the Kevin Keegan era with a magnificent hat-trick. Only five of the team which scraped home in Luxembourg survive the shake-up as Keegan launches a more positive approach to international football. His tactics are an overwhelming success with a sell-out Wembley crowd, who sense the Euro 2000 challenge is back on track. Scholes, who has never scored a hat-trick at senior level for Manchester United, admits: 'Life doesn't get better than this for me.'

GINGER GOALS...Scholes finds his shooting boots against Poland at Wembley.

England 3   Poland 1
(Scholes 3)   (Brzeczek)

27 March 1999, Wembley
ENGLAND: Seaman, G.Neville, Le Saux, Sherwood, Keown, Campbell, Beckham (P.Neville 78), Scholes (Redknapp 83), Shearer, Cole, McManaman (Parlour 70).
POLAND: Matysek, Hajto, Zielinski, Lapinski, Ratajczyk, Swierczewski (Klos 46), Bak, Brzeczek, Siadaczka (Kowalczyk 68), Iwan, Trzeciak (Juskowiak 83).

HONEYMOON OVER... Keegan realises he's got a tough time ahead after failing to put away the Swedes at Wembley.

England 0 Sweden 0

5 June 1999, Wembley

ENGLAND: Seaman, P.Neville, Le Saux (Gray 46), Batty, Keown (Ferdinand 34), Campbell, Beckham (Parlour 75), Sherwood, Shearer, Cole, Scholes.

SWEDEN: Hedman, Nilsson, Kamark, Schwarz, P.Andersson, Bjorklund, Mild (Alexandersson 6), Mjallby (D.Andersson 82), K.Andersson, Larsson (Svensson 69), Ljungberg.

It's back to the drawing board for Keegan as Sweden get the point they need to virtually wrap up their place at Euro 2000. England are totally lacking in ideas, movement and creativity against disciplined but far from outstanding opponents. It could have been even worse for England after Paul Scholes becomes the first England player ever to be sent off at Wembley. But the cautious Swedes are happy to sit back and defend for the remaining 39 minutes, settling for the draw they came for.

Things are starting to look positively bleak as Keegan admits for the first time that England might not even make the play-offs. Despite six changes to the side held four days earlier by Sweden, there is little sign of improvement in Sofia as Keegan's men run out of ideas again. Even when Alan Shearer fires England into a 15th minute lead, England are only able to hold their advantage for three minutes before conceding a scrappy equaliser. Bulgarian sub Milen Petrov is sent off with 30 minutes remaining, but England fail to capitalise on their numerical advantage. Poland's 3-2 win in Luxembourg on the same night leaves them three points clear in second place.

Bulgaria 1   England 1
(Markov)   (Shearer)

9 June 1999, Sofia
BULGARIA: Ivankov, Kirilov, Stoilov, Kishishev, Zagorcic, Markov, S.Petrov, Iliev (Borimirov 60), M Petkov, Stoichkov (Bachev 73), Yovov (M.Petrov 46).
ENGLAND: Seaman, P.Neville, Gray, Southgate, Woodgate (Parlour 64), Campbell, Redknapp, Batty, Shearer, Fowler (Heskey 81), Sheringham.

England 6   Luxembourg 0
(Shearer 3, McManaman 2, Owen)

4 September 1999, Wembley
ENGLAND: Martyn, Dyer (G.Neville 46), Pearce, Batty, Adams (P.Neville 64), Keown, Beckham (Owen 64), Parlour, Shearer, Fowler, McManaman.
LUXEMBOURG: Felgen, Ferron, Schauls, Birsens, Funck, Saibene, Theis, Vanek, Christophe (Zaritski 61), Schneider (Alverdi 46), Posing (F.Deville).

Something to shout about at last as Alan Shearer's first-half hat-trick and the first goals of Steve McManaman's international career suggest that at least England intend to go down fighting. Yet even the prospect of a morale-boosting goal glut is squandered as England lose their way after the break and fail to add to the scoresheet until Michael Owen's last minute strike. Keegan insists his troops are in good

spirits for the make or break visit to Poland four days later. This result does little to alter England's Championship prospects.

Final Group 5 table

	P	W	D	L	F	A	Pts
Sweden	8	7	1	0	10	1	22
England	8	3	4	1	14	4	13
Poland	8	4	1	3	12	8	13
Bulgaria	8	2	2	4	6	8	8
Luxembourg	8	0	0	8	2	23	0

Poland 0   England 0

8 September 1999, Warsaw

POLAND: Matysek, Klos (Bak 89), Waldoch, Siadaczka, Zielinski, Hajto, Michalski, Iwan, Gilewicz (Juskowiak 59), Nowak, Trzeciak (Swierczewski 59).

ENGLAND: Martyn, G.Neville (P.Neville 13), Pearce, Batty, Adams, Keown, Beckham, Scholes, Shearer, Fowler (Owen 66), McManaman (Dyer 70).

FOWL UP...Robbie wastes a chance as England scramble a point in Warsaw.

England are still hanging on by a thread but it's looking bleak after the third goalless draw of their qualifying campaign. Victory for either team would have guaranteed their play-off place, but nerves get the better of everyone on another night to forget. England are convinced they should have had two penalties for fouls on Alan Shearer and Paul Scholes but are left clinging on for a point when David Batty is sent off for a ludicrous late challenge. Now Poland must lose their final match in Sweden if England are to make the play-offs. 'It's fingers crossed for the whole nation,' Keegan admits. 'I didn't want to qualify for the finals like this, but if Sweden can throw us a lifeline we'll take it.'

Group 1 table

	P	W	D	L	F	A	Pts
Italy	**8**	**4**	**3**	**1**	**13**	**5**	**15**
Denmark	**8**	**4**	**2**	**2**	**11**	**8**	**14**
Switzerland	8	4	2	2	9	5	14
Wales	8	3	0	5	7	16	9
Belarus	8	0	3	5	4	10	3

Group 1

ITALIANS FAIL TO IMPRESS

Italy did their best to mess up but in the end just avoided the play-offs courtesy of a goalless draw in Belarus in their final group game. But their unimpressive qualifying record, winning only 50 per cent of their games in a seemingly straight-forward group, counted against the Italians when it came to the Euro 2000 seedings. Denmark, who managed just two points from their first four games, came from nowhere to snatch runners-up spot from the Swiss thanks to a remarkable 3-2 win in Italy in their last game. The Danes then hammered Israel 8-0 on aggregate in the play-offs to ensure their place at the finals.

Group 2

ONE WAY TRAFFIC FOR NORWEGIANS

Norway won at a stroll in what was probably the easiest of all nine qualifying groups, taking maximum points from their final seven games. Yet they had to recover from a nightmare start when they lost at home to Latvia then scored twice in the last eight minutes to scrape a home draw with Albania. Surprise package of the group were Slovenia, who pipped Greece to the runners-up spot then beat the highly-rated Ukranians in the play-offs.

Group 3

TURKS GIVE GERMANS A FRIGHT

Germany's place at the top of the table was no surprise to anyone. The big shock was the form of Turkey, who ran them all the way and would have won the group but for a costly home defeat by

Group 2 table

	P	W	D	L	F	A	Pts
Norway	**10**	**8**	**1**	**1**	**21**	**9**	**25**
Slovenia	**10**	**5**	**2**	**3**	**12**	**14**	**17**
Greece	10	4	3	3	13	8	15
Latvia	10	3	4	3	13	12	13
Albania	10	1	4	5	8	14	7
Georgia	10	1	2	7	8	18	5

Group 3 table

	P	W	D	L	F	A	Pts
Germany	8	6	1	1	20	4	19
Turkey	8	5	2	1	15	6	17
Finland	8	3	1	4	13	13	10
N Ireland	8	1	2	5	4	19	5
Moldova	8	0	4	4	7	17	4

Group 4 table

	P	W	D	L	F	A	Pts
France	10	6	3	1	17	10	21
Ukraine	10	5	5	0	14	4	20
Russia	10	6	1	3	22	12	19
Iceland	10	4	3	3	12	7	15
Armenia	10	2	2	6	8	15	8
Andorra	10	0	0	10	3	28	0

Finland early in their qualifying campaign. Germany, having lost their opening game in Bursa, only needed to avoid defeat in the return match in Munich last October. A goalless draw was enough to keep the Turks in second place, but Mustafa Denizli's men confirmed their dark horse status by defeating the Republic of Ireland in the play-offs.

Group 4

THREE-WAY CHALLENGE AT THE TOP

With three potential Euro 2000 winners in a six-nation qualifying group, this was always going to be mighty close. Even World champions France couldn't take their place in the finals for granted, particularly after a 3-2 home defeat by the Russians last June. Going into the final day of the qualifiers, 9 October, France were third in the group. But a nervous 3-2 home win against Iceland, coupled with Russia's 1-1 draw with the Ukraine in Moscow, was enough for Roger Lemerre's men to snatch first place. The Ukranians, shattered to find themselves in the play-offs, failed to pull themselves together in time and were dumped by little Slovenia.

Group 6 table

	P	W	D	L	F	A	Pts
Spain	8	7	0	1	42	5	21
Israel	8	4	1	3	25	9	13
Austria	8	4	1	3	19	20	13
Cyprus	8	4	0	4	12	21	12
San Marino	8	0	0	8	1	44	0

score an amazing 40 goals in their next seven games. Superstar striker Raul was responsible for 11 of those, including seven in four days against Austria and San Marino. Israel, who had briefly led the group, finished a distant second but flopped dismally in the play-offs and were hammered out of sight by Denmark.

Group 7

UNBEATEN ROMANIA EDGE IT

Romania and Portugal, two evenly matched teams, were in a class of their own in Group 7 and it was always going to be a heated personal battle for supremacy. Romania, who started with a 7-0 thrashing of whipping boys Liechtenstein, remained unbeaten throughout and just edged home by a single point. But in the end it was all academic as Portugal were able to avoid the play-offs and gain automatic entry to Euro 2000 by finishing as the second place team with the best record.

Group 6

RAUL INSPIRES GOAL HUNGRY SPANIARDS

A personal triumph for Spanish coach Jose Antonio Camacho, who took over from Javier Clemente after the shock 3-2 defeat in Cyprus then saw his team

Group 7 table

	P	W	D	L	F	A	Pts
Romania	10	7	3	0	25	3	24
Portugal	10	7	2	1	32	4	23
Slovakia	10	5	2	3	12	9	17
Hungary	10	3	3	4	14	10	12
Azerbaijan	10	1	1	8	6	26	4
Liechtenstein	10	1	1	8	2	39	4

Group 8

IRISH FAIL IN BALKANS BATTLE

With three nations from the former Yugoslavia overshadowed by the Balkans War, there were real fears that this group might not even be completed. Yugoslavia, the subject of NATO bombings at the time, needed UEFA's assistance to fulfil all their fixtures and remarkably took the group with a final day draw away to bitter rivals Croatia. The Republic of Ireland, held to a costly draw in Macedonia on the same day, fancied their chances in the play-offs but failed after two ill-tempered clashes with the Turks.

Group 9

CZECHS SWEEP ALL BEFORE THEM

A virtual stroll in the park for the Czechs, the only team to boast a perfect, one hundred per cent qualifying record. In one of the easiest of Euro 2000 groups, Jozef Chovanec's team had it all wrapped up with three games still to play. They might not find life quite so easy against France, Holland and Denmark in 'The Group of Death'. Scotland's place in the play-offs was never really in doubt but Craig Brown's team fluffed their lines in the first leg against England and recovered their form too late to make up the deficit.

Group 8 table

	P	W	D	L	F	A	Pts
Yugoslavia	8	5	2	1	18	8	17
Rep. of Ireland	8	5	1	2	14	6	16
Croatia	8	4	3	1	13	9	15
Macedonia	8	2	2	4	13	14	8
Malta	8	0	0	8	6	27	0

Group 9 table

	P	W	D	L	F	A	Pts
Czech Republic	10	10	0	0	26	5	30
Scotland	10	5	3	2	15	10	18
Lithuania	10	3	2	5	8	16	11
Estonia	10	3	2	5	15	17	11
Bosnia-Herzegovina	10	3	2	5	14	17	11
Faroe Isles	10	0	3	7	4	17	3

Play-off results

Scotland	0	England	2	Slovenia	2	Ukraine	1
England	0	Scotland	1	Ukraine	1	Slovenia	1
England qualify 2-1 on aggregate				Slovenia qualify 3-2 on aggregate			
Israel	0	Denmark	5	Rep. of Ireland	1	Turkey	1
Denmark	3	Israel	0	Turkey	0	Rep Ireland	0
Denmark qualify 8-0 on aggregate				Aggregate 1-1. Turkey qualify on away goals			

Scholes puts Scotland to the sword

When UEFA inadvertently revived the oldest international fixture in football they stirred up more than 125 years of pride, passion and pure hatred.

It was in the unlikely setting of Aachen that the Euro 2000 play-off draw threw England and Scotland onto a collision course. The impact could be heard across Europe as a match abandoned for security reasons ten years earlier was suddenly turned into a winner-takes-all confrontation.

England, after a dismal qualifying campaign, had sneaked into the equation courtesy of Sweden's victory over Poland which handed Kevin Keegan's team second place in Group 5. Scotland's place in the play-offs had been a much more relaxed affair. They finished a comfortable second in Group 9 behind runaway winners the Czech Republic. Yet, right from the start, Kevin Keegan was boldly predicting his team would go through and even suggested they could go on to win the Championships. Scotland coach Craig Brown was far more cautious, pointedly talking down his team's chances while consciously building up the opposition. For an entire month the country was engrossed by 'The Battle of Britain'. Everyone had an opinion on the big match. And nobody gave Scotland a prayer.

England's superiority complex had been prompted by their comfortable victory when the teams last met. Gary McAllister's penalty miss and Paul Gascoigne's Wembley wonder goal had combined to give England

BREAKTHROUGH...Scholes nets the first of his two goals.

THREE AMIGOS... Owen, Redknapp and Ince reflect on a job well done.

a crucial Euro 96 victory. Even the most hardened member of the Tartan Army was hard pressed to predict that Scotland would fare much better this time.

England fans, far from overwhelmed by their own team's recent form, were mystified by such Scottish pessimism. Yet all became clear at Hampden Park on Saturday 13 November as Keegan's men claimed a seemingly unassailable first-leg lead. Two goals from Paul Scholes were more than enough to silence the

Scotland 0	England 2
	(Scholes 2)

13 November 1999, Hampden Park, att 50,132
SCOTLAND: Sullivan, Weir, Ritchie, Dailly, Hendry, Ferguson, Dodds, Burley, Gallacher (Burchill 82), Hutchison, Collins
ENGLAND: Seaman, Campbell, P.Neville, Ince, Adams, Keown, Beckham, Scholes, Shearer, Owen (Cole 67), Redknapp.

Hampden Roar and leave England in total control of the tie.

Brown's policy of basing the nucleus of his team around Scottish-based players had backfired badly as his team failed to rise to the occasion. Smug English followers lapped it up, with many even suggesting that Scotland should do themselves a favour and not bother coming down to Wembley for the return leg.

Yet their confidence was to prove foolishly premature and four days later it was England who were left humiliated on their own turf. Scotland, sensing they had nothing to lose, threw off their first-leg caution and took the game to the Auld Enemy. Their positive approach clearly shocked Keegan and his team and Don Hutchison's 39th minute header left England clinging on for dear life. Scotland, discerning one of the most sensational comebacks of all time, battered England senseless and only David Seaman's

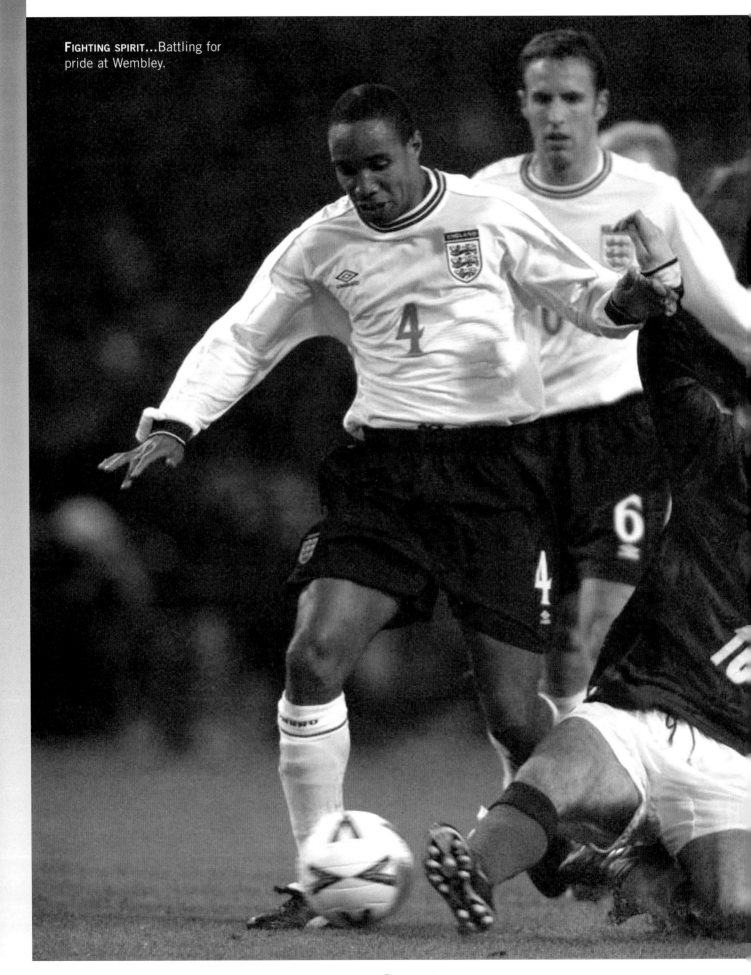

FIGHTING SPIRIT... Battling for pride at Wembley.

point blank late save from Christian Dailly denied them the extra-time their efforts deserved.

A disappointed Brown admitted: 'Everyone said we were just here to beat England but our job was to qualify for the European Championships and we have failed. The bottom line is that we're out of Euro 2000 and I feel really gutted about that.'

A relieved Keegan added: 'At least we're in the finals and I've got a bit of leeway to get things right before the summer. That is the only consolation for me. People might laugh, but at least we now have the chance to do well on the big stage.'

Keegan, the eternal optimist, knows he has his work cut out to get his squad into fighting shape for Euro 2000. At least Scotland's unheralded heroes have given the England coach a more realistic view of his team's chances in Belgium and Holland.

PARTY POOPER... Don Hutchison's goal gives England more than a fright.

England 0   Scotland 1
(Hutchison)

17 November 1999, Wembley, att 75,848
ENGLAND: Seaman, Campbell, P.Neville, Ince, Adams, Southgate, Beckham, Scholes (Parlour 90), Shearer, Owen (Heskey 63), Redknapp.
SCOTLAND: Sullivan, Weir, Davidson, Dailly, Hendry, Ferguson, Dodds, Burley, McCann (Burchill 74), Hutchison, Collins.

'JUST' MISSED OUT... Just Fontaine missed France's vital semi-final clash with the Yugoslavs at Euro 60.

France 1960

The European Championships were a long time in the coming. They were first proposed by Frenchman Henri Delaunay in 1927, but it was not for another 50 years that the concept was given the go-ahead by UEFA.

Delaunay's vision of a European tournament was in direct opposition to Jules Rimet's ideas for a World Cup. But his argument for greater ease of travel and communication were outvoted by FIFA's executive committee, who were fired by visions of a global competition. It wasn't until the formation of UEFA in 1954 that serious thought was given to a showdown for Europe's best nations. The European Nations' Cup was finally agreed in August 1957, two years after Delaunay's death.

The magnificent silver trophy awarded to the winners was named after the visionary Frenchman. Yet initial reaction to the new competition was decidely lukewarm. Of UEFA's original 29 members, only 14 voted in favour of a European Championships. Seven were against, five (including England, Scotland and Northern Ireland) abstained and three didn't even bother to attend the meeting in Copenhagen.

Seventeen nations entered the first European Championships. One week was set aside for the semi-finals, third-place play-off and final and the tournament was awarded to France in recognition of Delaunay's contribution. Among the notable absentees were England, Italy and West Germany. The first match took place in Moscow on 28 September 1958 when the USSR beat Hungary 3-1 in the first leg of their first round clash. Anatoly Ilyin had the distinction of scoring the very first goal.

The sniffy attitude and non-participation of many of Europe's super powers was not UEFA's only problem. When Spain were drawn against the USSR in the quarter-finals, General Franco refused to allow the Soviets into the country because of their role in the Spanish civil war 20 years earlier. UEFA had no option but to award the tie to the Russians. France were overwhelming favourites to be the first winners of the Henri Delaunay Cup after scoring eight against Greece in the first round and nine in the quarter-finals against Austria. Yet they had not reckoned on the incredible fighting spirit of the Yugoslavs in Paris.

Even without the injured Just Fontaine and Raymond Kopa, France seemed destined for the final as they swept into a 4-2 lead in the Parc des Princes. But three goals in as many minutes from the Yugoslavs turned the semi-final on its head and provided the Championships with a far from glamorous Iron Curtain final. Less than 18,000 fans turned out to see the Soviet Union crowned the first kings of Europe. Yugoslavia had taken the lead shortly before half-time

10 July 1960, Parc des Princes, Paris, att 17,966

**USSR 2 (Metrevelli 49, Ponedelnik 113)
Yugoslavia 1 (Galic 41) aet**

USSR: Yashin, Chekheli, Maslenkin, Krutikov, Voinov, Netto, Metrevelli, Ivanov, Ponedelnik, Bubukhin, Meshki

Yugoslavia: Vidinic, Durkovic, Miladinovic, Jusufi, Zanetic, Perusic, Matus, Jerkovic, Galic, Sekularac, Kostic

with a header from Milan Galic which went in with the aid of a deflection off Soviet skipper Igor Netto. But they were unable to cash in on their superiority, with Lev Yashin in magnificent form in the Russian goal.

When Slava Metrevelli levelled against the run of play in the 50th minute, the Yugoslavs started to wilt and with the final going into extra-time there was only going to be one winner. Soviet striker Viktor Ponedelnik duly headed his nation's winning goal.

Spain 1964!

England, at last convinced that the Championships did not pose a threat to the future of the Home Internationals, finally deigned to join the rest of Europe for the second Nations' Cup.

OLE...Spain and their victorious manager take the plaudits at the Bernabeu.

Their challenge lasted just two games and provided a shock introduction to international football for new manager Alf Ramsey. The former Ipswich boss was named successor to Walter Winterbottom following a 1-1 first round draw with the French at Wembley. In his first game in charge, Ramsey's team were thrashed 5-2 in Paris in March 1963. West Germany, protesting at the number of their top players being lured to Italy, again refused to enter. Scotland were also missing, but they were the only major absentees among the 29 competitors.

Considering Franco's attitude to the communist nations in general and the defending Soviet champions

in particular, UEFA took a major gamble when they awarded Euro 64 to the Spaniards. But the Spanish government vowed that the tournament would not be disrupted by politics again, and they proved as good as their word when both the Russians and Hungarians qualified for the semi-finals in Barcelona and Madrid.

The USSR, one of three nations given a first round bye, had already accounted for the highly-rated Italians and Sweden on their way to the last four. Hungary had taken care of Wales, East Germany and, most notably, the French. But Spanish hopes of a home victory were high, with new coach Jose Villalonga largely ignoring the superstar reputations of Barcelona and Real Madrid and building his team around less celebrated players. His gamble almost came a cropper in the second round, when they were held to a 1-1 draw in Bilbao by Northern Ireland. UEFA were facing the nightmare scenario of their biggest competition taking place without the presence of the host nation. But Spain spared their blushes when they edged through the return leg 1-0 in Belfast with a goal from Francisco Gento.

The Republic of Ireland proved far easier opposition in the quarter-finals and Spain were joined in the last four by Denmark, who had needed a play-off to beat little Luxembourg in the previous round. The Danes proved no match for the mighty Soviets in the semi-final, going down 3-0 in Barcelona. But at least they could boast the tournament's top scorer in eleven-goal striker Ole Madsen.

Spain, swept along on a tide of nationalist fervour, were proving to be irresistible. Inspired by the return of former European Footballer of the Year Luis Suarez from Inter Milan, they proved too strong for Hungary in their Madrid semi and won 2-1 thanks to an extra-time winner from Amancio.

Five years after being refused entry to Spanish soil, the Soviets were back to face their bitter rivals in the European Championship final. 120,000 Spaniards

---

21 June 1964, Bernabeu Stadium, Madrid, att 120,000

Spain 2 (Pereda 6, Marcelino 83) USSR 1 (Khusainov 8)

Spain: Iribar, Rivilla, Calleja, Fuste, Olivella, Zoco, Amancio, Pereda, Marcelino, Suarez, Lapetra
USSR: Yashin, Shustikov, Shesternev, Mudrik, Voronin, Anichkin, Chislenko, Ivanov, Ponedelnik, Korneyev, Khusainov

crammed into the Bernabeu Stadium to witness the event. Franco, watching from the VIP box, could barely conceal his delight as the communist challenge was crushed in front of his eyes. Jesus Pereda gave Spain an early lead and though the Soviets grabbed an unexpected equaliser from Khusainov, they were merely delaying the inevitable. Marcelino put them out of their misery seven minues from time, triggering incredible scenes of celebration to mark what remains Spain's only major soccer triumph.

Italy 1968

Ten years after the introduction of the European Nations' Cup, the tournament's only black mark was finally eradicated when West Germany ditched their one-nation boycott and jumped onto the championship bandwagon.

The Germans, beaten World Cup finalists in England two years earlier, realised they could no longer afford to stay aloof if they were to maintain their stance as one of the major powers of world football. UEFA, who had officially retitled their competition as the European Championship, could not have done more to accommodate the newcomers.

In the corner...Bobby Charlton (out of shot) scores England's winner against the Spanish at Wembley.

With 31 of their 33 member nations entering the championships — only Malta and Iceland were missing — UEFA decided to scrap the traditional first round ties and organise eight qualifying groups instead.

Eight nations — England, Spain, Italy, West Germany, France, Portugal, the USSR and Hungary — were seeded. The Germans, riding their luck, were drawn in the only three-team group. Even so, Beckenbauer and his chums still managed to mess it up by drawing their final game 0-0 against lowly Albania and allowing Yugoslavia to snatch the quarter-final place.

UEFA had already decided that the Home Internationals were a ready-made qualifying group. England, the reigning world champions, duly won through despite Scotland's famous 3-2 Wembley win in 1967. Of the other seeded nations, only Portugal failed to reach the quarter-finals. They finished a distant third in their group behind Bulgaria and Sweden. Holland's opening game, a 2-2 draw with Hungary, was notable for the first international goal of a young Johann Cruyff, while Austria's home match with Greece was abandoned four minutes from the end following a pitch invasion.

Italy, still smarting from their shock World Cup defeat by North Korea in 1966, were desperate to reach the semi-final stage on home soil. A qualifying group containing Switzerland, Cyprus and Romania presented few problems for a squad totally overhauled by new coach Ferruccio

8 June 1968 Olympic Stadium, Rome, att 85,000.

Italy 1 (Domenghini 80) Yugoslavia 1 (Dzajic 39) aet
Italy: Zoff, Castano, Burgnich, Guarneri, Facchetti, Ferrini, Juliano, Lodetti, Domenghini, Anastasi, Prati
Yugoslavia: Pantelic, Fazlagic, Holcer, Paunovic, Damjanovic, Acimovic, Trivic, Pavlovic, Petkovic, Musemic, Dzajic

REPLAY

10 June 1968, Olympic Stadium, Rome, att 50,000.

Italy 2 (Riva 11, Anastasi 32) Yugoslavia 0
Italy: Zoff, Salvadore, Burgnich, Guarneri, Facchetti, Rosato, De Sisti, Domenghini, Mazzola, Anastasi, Riva
Yugoslavia: Pantelic, Fazlagic, Paunovic, Holcer, Damjanovic, Acimovic, Trivic, Pavlovic, Hosic, Musemic, Dzajic

Valcareggi. Yet they almost came a cropper in the two-legged quarter-finals against Bulgaria, losing 3-2 in Sofia before salvaging the situation with a 2-0 home victory in the return. Yugoslavia and the Soviet Union also won through to the last four but the pick of the quarter-finals was undoubtedly world champions England against European champs Spain.

Bobby Charlton gave England a 1-0 victory at Wembley and though Amancio quickly levelled the aggregate scores in the return leg, further goals from Martin Peters and Norman Hunter gave England a famous victory in Madrid. But that was where their luck ran out. Their semi-final clash with Yugoslavia in Florence ended in a disappointing 1-0 defeat. Alan Mullery became the first England player ever to be sent-off. Italy, becoming more cautious the further they progressed, needed the toss of a coin to settle the semi-final clash with the USSR in their favour following a goalless draw.

The Final, in Rome's Olympic Stadium, was another stalemate. Angelo Domenghini cancelled out Dragan Dzajic's 39th minute goal for Yugoslavia and the Italians then decided to put up the shutters throughout extra-time. The replay, two days later, was too much for the shattered Slavs. Riva and Anastasi made sure there was no Roman respite for them.

Belgium 1972

No nation has ever dominated the European Championships as much as the West Germans did in 1972. Helmut Schoen's team were streets ahead of the 31 other countries and their margin of victory in the final was the biggest in the tournament's 40-year history. Four years after their shock failure to qualify for the final stages, the Germans made sure there were absolutely no mistakes this time. Despite drawing their opening game at home to Turkey, they cruised through Group 8 to book their quarter-final place at a stroll.

They were joined in the last eight by Romania, Hungary, England, the USSR, Belgium, Italy and Yugoslavia. England were relatively untroubled in a group also containing Greece, Switzerland and Malta. Spurs striker Martin Chivers scored five goals in six games to ensure Sir Alf Ramsey's team finished two points clear of the field.

Defending champions Italy were equally comfortable in their group games but 1964 winners Spain missed out this time, finishing two points behind their old Soviet adversaries. Once again the quarter-finals were played over two legs, with England against West Germany the obvious tie of the round. England had famously triumphed when they met in the 1966 World Cup final at Wembley, but the Germans prevailed four years later in Mexico, fighting back from 2-0 down to claim a memorable World Cup quarter-final victory.

Ramsey's team hoped to strike a decisive blow in the first leg of their clash at Wembley, in April 1972. But they were simply overwhelmed by the brilliance of the Germans, with skipper Franz Beckenbauer and midfield playmaker Gunter Netzer virtually

18 June 1972, Heysel Stadium, Brussels, att 50,000.

W Germany 3 (Muller 27 58, Wimmer 52) USSR 0
W Germany: Maier, Hottges, Schwarzenbeck, Beckenbauer, Breitner, Hoeness, Netzer, Wimmer, Heynckes, Muller, Kremers
USSR: Rudakov, Dzodzuashvili, Khurtsilava, Kaplichni, Istomin, Troshkin, Kolotov, Konkov (Dolmatov 46), Baidachni, Banishevski (Kozenkevich 66), Onishenko

unstoppable. Goals from Uli Hoeness, Gerd Muller and a Netzer penalty effectively ended England's interest in the competition. Although Francis Lee pulled one back before the end, the tie was as good as over and a goalless draw in Berlin two weeks later confirmed Germany's place in the semi-finals.

Elsewhere, Italy's grip on the trophy was ended by Belgium, who were subsequently awarded the final stages of the tournament by UEFA. The USSR crushed Yugoslavia 3-0 in Moscow following a goalless draw in Belgrade while Hungary beat Romania in a play-off following two draws. The semi-finals, played on the same day and less than 100 miles apart, could not have offered greater contrast. In Brussels, just 3,500 supporters turned out to see a functional but unspectacular Soviet side beat the Hungarians 1-0. It was the third time in four European Championships that the Russians had reached the final. Later that day, Antwerp witnessed a 60,000 lock-out for Belgium's clash with the Germans. Home expectations were high, sparked by the presence of the brilliant Paul Van Himst, probably the greatest player in Belgian history. But even he could not stem the German tide and two more goals from the peerless Muller were enough to take Schoen's men through.

SCHOEN SHINE IN BELGIUM...Helmut's Schoen's German side totally dominated the 1972 Championships.

The final, staged at the ill-fated Heysel Stadium, was to prove even more one-sided. The Russians had no answer to the relentless surge of German pressure and once Muller had struck in the 27th minute they were never at the races. Herbert Wimmer struck a second German goal seven minutes after the break and Muller confirmed Germany's superiority five minutes later with his 11th goal of the Championships.

Yugoslavia 1976

When Czechoslovakia lost 3-0 at Wembley in the opening match of their 1976 European Championship campaign, there was little to suggest that they were about to embark on a 23-match unbeaten run which would eventually see them crowned kings of football's most powerful continent. Yet from that unlikely beginning, an unheralded team put together by Vaclav Jezek and Jozef Venglos emerged triumphant in one of the most thrilling tournaments in the history of the Euros.

The turning point for the Czechs can be traced back to October 1975, when they came from a goal behind to defeat England 2-1 in the return qualifying match in Bratislava, a day after the match had been abandoned due to fog. England were never able to recover from that setback and finished a point behind the Czechs in Group One.

Yet British interest was maintained by Wales' shock success in Group Two, where goals from John Toshack and John Mahoney gave them a famous victory in Budapest and allowed them to finish three points clear of group favourites Hungary. Also through to the quarter-finals for the first time were the brilliant Holland team who, inspired by Cruyff, Neeskens and Krol, had played the Germans in the World Cup final two years earlier. They won through at the expense of Italy and Poland, despite losing away to both teams, and were widely tipped to give the reigning World and European champions a real run for their money.

Yugoslavia, Spain, Russia, Belgium and, inevitably, West Germany completed the quarter-final line-up. Sadly for the Welsh, that was far as they were going. Yugoslavia beat them 2-0 in Belgrade, drew 1-1 in

20 June 1976, Red Star Stadium, Belgrade, att 33,000.
Czechoslovakia 2 (Svehlik 8, Dobias 25)
W Germany 2 (Muller D 28, Holzenbein 89) aet,
Czechoslovakia won 5-3 on penalties
Czechoslovakia: Viktor, Pivarnik, Ondrus, Capkovic, Gogh, Dobias (Vesely 94), Panenka, Moder, Masny, Svehlik (Jurkemik 79), Nehoda
W Germany: Maier, Vogts, Beckenbauer, Schwarzenbeck, Dietz, Wimmer (Flohe 46), Bonhof, Beer (Bongartz 79), Hoeness, D Muller, Holzenbein

MR COOL...Antonin Panenka's audacious penalty booked him a place in football folklore.

Cardiff and were then awarded the final stages of the tournament by UEFA. Holland confirmed their status as the rising stars of Europe by thrashing neighbours Belgium 7-1 on aggregate, the Germans beat Spain and the Czechs continued to upset the apple cart by knocking out the USSR. But it wasn't until the semi-finals that the tournament really caught fire.

Holland and West Germany were odds on favourites to face each other again in the final, but the Czechs had other ideas. Even Holland's famous 'total football' could not break down Jezek's well organised defence in Zagreb. The match was poised on a knife edge going into extra-time, but the sendings-off of Johan Neeskens and Wim Van Hanegem turned the tie Czechoslovakia's way and they went on to win 3-1.

Even the Germans were given the fright of their lives by Yugoslavia, trailing 2-0 before Dieter Muller's hat-trick set up a 4-2 victory. The young Cologne striker was proving a more than adequate replacement for his predecessor and namesake Gerd Muller. There is no doubt the Germans were no longer the force they had been four years earlier in Belgium. Yet they were still perceived as being infinitely superior to the Czechs. So when they fought back from a two-goal deficit to force the Belgrade final into extra-time, it seemed a simple case of 'here we go again'.

Yet fate was about to play a cruel trick on the Germans. And it was a trick of their own making. Just a day before the final, UEFA announced that there would be no replay in the event of a draw. The match would be settled by means of a new concept — the penalty shoot-out. The idea was purely a German one. They insisted on getting the final over quickly because they wanted their players to get as much rest as possible. The Czech players didn't even know about it. Yet when the shoot-out became a reality, it was the Germans who were totally unprepared.

Dietz and Schwarzenbeck flatly refused to be put on the spot and skipper Beckenbauer was forced to volunteer to take the vital fifth kick by the forceful Sepp Maier. He was never needed. For while the Czechs held their nerve and their aim, Uli Hoeness blasted Germany's fourth kick over the bar. Step forward Antonin Panenka to claim his place in football folklore with his outrageous chip beyond the already committed Maier.

Italy 1980

If Yugoslavia 76 had provided one of the greatest tournaments of football's history, then Italy 1980 was to prove a dreadful disappointment. Even the decision to increase the finals from four to eight teams failed to provide the spark needed to ignite an event dragged down by the negative, defensive attitude of nearly all the competing sides. Ron Greenwood's England were as guilty as anyone, although there had been little warning

MACHINE-LIKE...Another Championships, another victory for the relentless Germans in 1980.

of this sudden loss of courage during an impressive qualifying campaign in which they only dropped one point in eight games against Northern Ireland, the Republic of Ireland, Bulgaria and Denmark.

Because of the change to the competition's format, the host nation had to be decided well in advance. Italy were chosen, for the second time in 12 years, and were also handed an automatic place in the finals. That left 32 countries to scramble for the remaining seven places, with England eventually joined by Belgium, Spain, Holland, Czechoslovakia, Greece and West Germany. Between them those countries should have had more than enough talent and flair to justify UEFA's decision to expand their most prestigious event. But they didn't. Holders Czechoslovakia were fading rapidly, the Germans had waved goodbye to Beckenbauer and the Dutch were without Cruyff. Italy and Spain were brutally defensive in outlook and England's hopes that Kevin Keegan would emerge as the star of the tournament proved dismally short-lived.

In fact the abiding memory of England's contribution to the tournament was the behaviour of their hooligan followers and it was to a backdrop of tear gas that Greenwood's team played out an uninspired 1-1 draw with Belgium in their opening game in Turin. Because of the increase in numbers, the old quarter-finals and semi-finals had been scrapped and replaced with two mini-leagues of four teams. The winners of each group went straight through to the final. England, in with Belgium, Italy and Spain, believed they had a reasonable chance of going all the way. But a 1-0 defeat by the host nation in their next game, courtesy of Marco Tardelli's goal, ended their interest in the competition. Beating Spain 2-1 in their

BEST OF A BAD LOT... Germany were the winners of the dullest Championships in memory.

22 June 1980, Olympic Stadium, Rome, att 48,000.

W Germany 2 (Hrubesch 12, 89) **Belgium 1** (Vandereycken 72 pen)

W.Germany: Schumacher, Briegel (Cullman 55), Forster, Dietz, Schuster, Rummenigge, Hrubesch, Muller, Aloffs, Stielike, Kaltz

Belgium: Pfaff, Gerets, Millecamps, Meeuws, Renquin, Cools, Van der Eycken, Van Moer, Mommens, Van der Elst, Ceulemans

final group game with goals from Trevor Brooking and Tony Woodcock was purely academic.

Surprisingly, it was Belgium who topped the group, beating Spain 2-1 then capitalising on Italy's incredible lack of adventure to snatch a goalless draw in Rome. The other group promised much more, but delivered little. Only the meeting of old enemies Holland and West Germany lived up to expectations, with a magnificent Klaus Allofs hat-trick in Naples giving the Germans a decisive 3-2 victory. That left them needing only a point from their final group game against Greece to reach their third successive final. A goalless draw in Turin was sufficient.

Considering the disappointing nature of the tournament so far, it was hardly surprising that the Olympic Stadium was little more than half full for the final. Belgium briefly threatened to bring some life to the proceedings when Rene Vandereycken equalised in the 72nd minute from the penalty spot after Uli Stielike had tripped Francois Van der Elst. But Horst Hrubesch's second goal of the match, a last minute header from Karl-Heinz Rummenigge's corner, provided the German victory anticipated before a ball had even been kicked.

France 1984

The name of Michel Platini is indelibly stamped on the 1984 European Championship. From start to finish, the brilliant French captain was the most influential player of the tournament. As the host nation, the French did not need to go through the inconvenience of qualifying. Given the quality of their team at the time, there is no doubt that they would have topped any obstacle placed in their way. But

LE MAGNIFIQUE...Platini and team-mates (below) lap up the applause after the 1984 final.

there were plenty of football's super powers who did stumble on the road to France – most notably Holland, Italy and England.

Bobby Robson's team appeared to be well on course for qualification after drawing in Denmark, winning in Greece then thrashing Luxembourg 9-0. But the wheels came off their campaign in September 1983 when Allan Simonsen scored from the spot to give the Danes a priceless Wembley victory which enabled them to finish top of the group by a point. Simonsen, the former European Footballer of the Year, was undoubtedly a key player. Unfortunately, he broke his leg in the opening game of the finals and Denmark's chances went with him.

Italy, incredibly, finished fourth in their five-team group behind Romania, Sweden and Czechoslovakia,

SHOWTIME...Platini's incredible displays lit up the 1984 Championships and raised the profile of the tournament to the outside world.

but the shock of the qualifiers was undoubtedly Holland's controversial elimination by Spain. The two teams were neck and neck going into the last round of games but Holland's goal difference was infinitely superior and when they beat Malta 5-0 they assumed their place in the finals was safe. After all, the Spanish would have to win their last game against Malta by 11 goals to deny them. Four days later, quite incredibly, Spain won 12-1!

As at Italy four years earlier, the eight finalists were split into two groups. But this time the top two would advance into a knock-out semi-final stage. In Group One, there was never any doubt as to who would finish top of the pile. Platini set the bandwagon rolling with the winning goal against Denmark then annihilated Belgium and Yugoslavia with a hat-trick in each game. Denmark, who hammered Yugoslavia 5-0 in Lyon, also advanced to the last four.

Group Two was a much closer affair. Portugal booked their semi-final place with two draws and a 1-0 win against Romania. West Germany led the table going into the final match but were beaten 1-0 by Spain and missed out. It was to be Jupp Derwall's last match as German coach.

France were now on a roll. But it took a monumental effort to overcome the Portuguese in a magnificent semi-final in Marseilles, a match widely regarded as one of the greatest internationals of

all time. At 2-2 in the 29th minute of extra-time, the clash was just seconds away from a penalty shoot-out. Platini's eighth goal of the tournament saved his nation the uncertainty of spot kicks. No such luck in the other semi, where Spain edged out the Danes 5-4 on penalties following a 1-1 draw in Lyon. The team who had scored 12 goals in one game to reach France 84 had got to the Final without netting more than one in any of their four games. But their luck was about to run out in the Parc des Princes against a French team guided by their brilliant captain and supplemented by the talents of Jean Tigana, Alain Giresse and Bernard Lacombe.

Inevitably, it was Platini who struck the first blow of the Paris final. Though the French had full-back Yvon Le Roux sent-off late in the game, they were never under threat from the disappointing Spanish and confirmed their triumph in the final minute when Bruno Bellone made it 2-0.

West Germany 1988

Throughout the 1970s, Holland were known as the best team never to have won a major championships. Ten years after Cruyff, Neeskens and Krol, the Dutch unearthed a new trio of superstars to end their long wait. Ruud Gullit, Marco Van Basten and Frank Rijkaard had already established their reputations at club level in Dutch football and with AC Milan, who they had all joined in 1987. Their performances at Euro 88 elevated them to superstar status.

Gullit, the Dutch captain and reigning World Footballer of the Year, was the focal point of his national side. Yet even he was upstaged by striker Van Basten in West Germany. Holland had cruised through their qualifying campaign, dropping only two points in eight games against Greece, Poland, Hungary and Cyprus. Only Bobby Robson's England team had a better record as they cruised through to the finals past Yugoslavia, Turkey and Northern Ireland. Spain, Italy, the USSR, Denmark and the Republic of Ireland completed the line-up, the Irish reaching a major championship finals for the first time in their history.

England arrived at their German base full of confidence. Not only had they qualified in style, but they also possessed world-rated stars like Gary Lineker, Bryan Robson and Peter Shilton. Unfortunately, their optimism was to prove misplaced.

OUTCLASSED...Gullit, Van Basten and Rijkaard (pictured) were too strong for England in the group stage.

Things started badly for Robson when Ray Houghton headed an unlikely Irish winner in an otherwise undistinguished Stuttgart scrap. They rapidly deteriorated against Holland as England fell to a Van Basten hat-trick. A third successive defeat by the USSR merely compounded their misery.

That Van Basten trio was a personal triumph for the master marksman. After a series of injury problems in the run-up to the finals, he had lost his place in the side to John Bosman and only agreed to join the squad after some persuasive conversations with Cruyff. Bosman, who scored five in a qualifier against Cyrpus which was declared invalid and another three in the replayed match, was preferred by coach Rinus Michels for Holland's first game against the USSR. But a 1-0 defeat in Cologne convinced the veteran Dutch coach that changes were needed for the England game and Van Basten was unleashed to devastating effect.

Ireland, meanwhile, were going from strength to strength and a 1-1 draw with Russia left Jack

Charlton's team on the brink of the semi-finals. A point from their final game against the Dutch would have been enough, but Wim Kieft's late freakish header cruelly destroyed their dream. The other group was a more straightforward affair. Italy and West Germany drew their opening match in Dusseldorf then both beat Spain and Denmark to progress to the last four. Germany, who had triumphed as the host nation in the 1974 World Cup, were hoping that home advantage would see their unconvincing team through against the Dutch in the semi-finals. They even took the lead in Hamburg with a Lothar Matthaus penalty, but Ronald Koeman levelled with a spot kick of his own and Van Basten struck in the final minute to deservedly take the Dutch through to the final.

The young Italian team, led by striker Gianluca Vialli, also ran out of steam one stage short of the final and never seriously troubled an underrated Soviet team, who won 2-0 in Stuttgart. The USSR, though, were to prove no match for Holland in the final and the absence of suspended Oleg Kuznetsov made little difference to the final outcome. Gullit headed the

25 June 1988, Olympic Stadium, Munich, att 72,308.

Holland 2 (Gullit 32, Van Basten 53) USSR 0

Holland: Van Breukelen, Van Aerle, Van Tiggelen, Wouters, R.Koeman, Rijkaard, Vanenburg, Gullit, Van Basten, Muhren, E.Koeman

USSR: Dassayev, Khidiatulin, Aleinikov, Mikhailichenko, Litovchenko, Demianenko, Belanov, Gotsmanov (Baltacha), Protasov (Pasulko), Zavarov, Rats

RASTAMAN...Gullit and Holland ruled supreme at the 1988 Championships.

HEADS UP... Gullit and Voller clash during the semi-final.

Dutch into a 33rd minute lead before Van Basten's stupendous angled volley provided a fitting finale for the player of the tournament. Igor Belanov had a late penalty saved by Dutch keeper Hans Van Breukelen but the Russians were already a beaten team by then.

Sweden 1992

When UEFA decided to ban Yugoslavia from the 1992 European Championships, they inadvertently sowed the seeds for one of the greatest sporting upsets of all time. With the Balkan War raging, UEFA ruled that the Yugoslavs presented too much of a security risk to attend the finals in decidedly neutral Sweden. Some of the most exciting young talents in Europe — including Suker, Boban, Prosinecki, Savicevic and

Jarni — were denied the opportunity to shine. Two weeks before the finals kicked off, their place was handed to the Danes, who had finished a point behind Yugoslavia in the qualifiers. And what a tale they had in store. Danish coach Richard Moller Nielsen was actually decorating his kitchen when he heard the news. He had to track down his players from the various beaches of Europe where they were enjoying their holidays.

England, their first opponents in Malmo, had problems of their own. Graham Taylor's team had been distinctly unimpressive in their qualifying campaign, scoring only seven goals in six games and requiring a late Gary Lineker equaliser to avert disaster in their final game in Poland. Injuries to Paul Gascoigne, John Barnes and Mark Wright before the tournament kicked off left Taylor's plans in disarray and dismal goalless draws against Denmark and France in their opening games of the tournament heaped on the pressure. They still had a chance to make the last four, though, and seemed to be in charge against hosts Sweden thanks to an early David Platt goal. But goals froms Eriksson and Brolin pushed England through the exit door and prompted *The Sun* to famously launch 'Turnip' Taylor.

Denmark, too, were in trouble following a 1-0 defeat by the Swedes. Their lack of preparation was apparently taking its toll until they unexpectedly hit form against Michel Platini's underachieving French team, who had won all eight of their qualifying games and boasted Jean-Pierre Papin and Eric Cantona up front. Lars Elstrup's winning goal was enough to take Denmark through into a semi-final showdown with

DANISH BUNDLE... John Jensen is mobbed by team-mates after opening the scoring in the Stockholm final at Euro 92.

PETER THE GREAT...A proud Schmeichel with the European trophy.

SENSATIONAL... Denmark triumph against all the odds on a night of fireworks.

Holland, whose new superstar striker Dennis Bergkamp had been on target in both wins against Scotland and Germany. Scotland, who had qualified for five successive World Cups but never the European Championships before, gave a more than decent account of themselves. They were never disgraced despite losing their first two games against the Dutch and Germans and enjoyed a comprehensive 3-0 win over a Soviet team masquerading under the name of the Commonwealth of Independent States.

The collapse of communism shortly before these championships might not have benefited the Soviet team, but it certainly helped the Germans, who were suddenly allowed to add former East German stars Matthias Sammer, Thomas Doll and Andreas Thom to their squad. On the minus side, injuries to Lothar Matthaus and Rudi Voller deprived them of their two most influential players, although they still had enough quality to end the Swedish dream in their

26 June 1992, Ullevi Stadium, Gothenburg, att 37,000.
Denmark 2 (Jensen 18, Vilfort 78) Germany 0
Denmark: Schmeichel, Siveback (Christiansen 66), Nielsen, Olsen, Christofte, Jensen, Povlsen, B. Laudrup, Piechnik, Larsen, Vilfort
Germany: Illgner, Reuter, Brehme, Kohler, Buchwald, Hassler, Riedle, Helmer, Sammer (Doll 46), Effenberg (Thom 80), Klinsmann

Stockholm semi-final, with Karl-Heinz Reidle scoring twice in a 3-2 win.

Holland, who had appeared unstoppable in their early games, paid the price for over-confidence in the other semi against a Danish team who were suddenly starting to believe that they were fated to win the championships. Ironically, it was Marco Van Basten, the Dutch hero of four years earlier, who missed the decisive penalty following a 2-2 draw in Gothenburg.

Germany, the most successful European nation in football, were overwhelming favourites to claim their third European Championships. But the Danes played like men inspired. To the delight of the Ullevi Stadium, goalkeeper Peter Schmeichel pulled off a series of superlative saves while John Jensen and Kim Vilfort scored the goals which confirmed Denmark's incredible triumph.

England 1996

It was supposed to be the year that football came home. Instead it went back to Germany. England's bid to host Euro 96 was guaranteed to succeed from the moment that UEFA decided to double the finals to take in 16 nations. England, with more than a dozen all-seater stadia already meeting the criteria, were probably the only country in Europe equipped to deal with such a tournament at short notice. The increase had been prompted by the sudden explosion of new nations created by the break up of the Eastern bloc countries. A record 48 teams entered for Euro 96, with Romania, France, Spain, Denmark, Switzerland, Turkey, Croatia, Italy, the Czech Republic, Holland, Portugal, Germany, Bulgaria, Russia and Scotland qualifying for the finals.

The last time England had hosted a tournament, they won the 1966 World Cup. But they entered these championships with their players under a cloud over boozing and coach Terry Venables announcing he would quit his job because of concerns over his business transactions. The opening game, a dull 1-1 draw with Switzerland, did little to inspire confidence in Venables' tactics. But Paul Gascoigne's splendid solo goal in England's next game, a thrilling 2-0 win against Scotland, was the signal for an incredible surge of patriotic fervour. A magnificent 4-1 demolition of the highly-rated Dutch guaranteed England top spot in their group and convinced the nation that England really were a world force once again. Patrick Kluivert's late consolation goal for Holland was to

GET THE BIERS IN... Oliver Bierhoff's double strike rescued the final for Germany.

HANDS UP...Klinsmann and co milk the applause.

prove crucial, denying Scotland a quarter-final place on goal difference.

France, benefiting from some basic defensive errors by Romania and Bulgaria, cruised through Group B pretty much untroubled and were joined in the last eight by Spain. Defending champions Denmark were bitterly disappointing in their group games and a crushing 3-0 defeat by Croatia effectively ended their hopes of maintaining their grip on the Henri Delaunay Cup. Portugal finished ahead of the Croats at the top of their first round group. But it was the so-called Group of Death — Germany, Italy, Russia and the Czech Republic — which was to provide most of the early shocks. Italy had looked so impressive in their opening win against the Russians that they rested half their team for their next game and were beaten 2-1 by the Czechs. That left them needing a result against leaders Germany in their final game at Old Trafford but Gianfranco Zola's penalty miss, combined with Vladimir Smicer's last-minute equaliser for the Czechs against Russia, sent the Italians packing.

The knock-out quarter-finals promised much but delivered little. The Czechs beat the unpredictable Portuguese 1-0 with a Karel Poborsky goal and Germany were 2-1 winners against Croatia with goals from Jurgen Klinsmann and Matthias Sammer. Holland failed to live up to expectations against France and even the introduction of the golden goal rule in extra-time failed to break the deadlock. In the end it needed Clarence Seedorf's miss to send the French through 5-4 on penalties. England against Spain also finished goalless, but David Seaman's penalty save from the luckless Miguel Angel Nadal kept the three lions bandwagon rolling towards a semi-final collision with the Germans.

For sheer drama, it was a contest probably unrivalled in the championship's history. Alan Shearer gave England a third minute lead with his fifth goal of the tournament and Stefan Kuntz levelled after quarter of an hour. The rest of the electrifying match, including extra-time, was nip and tuck all the way as two giants of the game slugged it out toe to toe. Inevitably, it needed another penalty shoot-out to separate the teams. And, of course, the Germans won. The Czech Republic, too, needed penalties to beat France after a goalless draw at Old Trafford. But their final meeting with the Germans was certain to be viewed as an anti-climax by a country which had worked itself into a frenzy over the possibility of an England triumph.

Only the possibility of a German defeat lured a sell-out crowd to Wembley for the final, and the Czechs did their best not to disappoint by taking the lead with a Patrik Berger penalty. But Oliver Bierhoff, surprisingly named among the subs by coach Berti Vogts, levelled within four minutes of replacing Mehmet Scholl then scored the first ever golden goal winner six minutes into extra-time.

GAZZAMANIA...An inspired Paul Gascoigne tormented the Dutch in England's final group game.

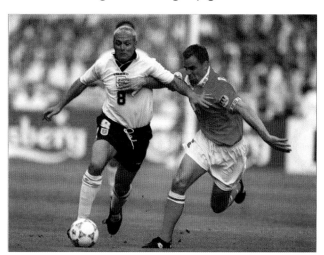

30 June 1996, Wembley Stadium, London, att 73,611

Germany 2 (Bierhoff 73, 95) Czech Republic 1 (Berger 59 pen)

Germany: Kopke, Babel, Sammer, Helmer, Strunz, Hassler, Eilts (Bode), Scholl (Bierhoff), Ziege, Klinsmann, Kuntz

Czech Republic: Kouba, Hornak, Rada, Kadlec, Suchoparek, Poborsky (Smicer), Nedved, Bejbl, Berger, Nemec, Kuka

FIVE MEMORABLE MATCHES

by Brian Woolnough, football correspondent, *The Sun*

YUGOSLAVIA 1 ENGLAND 0

5 June, 1968. Stadio Comunale,
Florence, Italy.

> **England Team:** Banks, Newton, Wilson, Mullery, Labone, Moore, Ball, Peters, R. Charlton, Hunt, Hunter.

This match will not just be remembered for England, the reigning World Champions, being knocked out in the semi-final. Alan Mullery became the first player to be sent off in an England shirt.

SHOWING HIS SPURS... Alan Mullery in happier times as an FA Cup winner with Tottenham.

This was also the match when Sir Alf, bless him, could not get his tongue around the Yugoslavian names in his pre-match team talk. He told his players to 'Be careful of Miloslav...o er.. and watch out for Dzaji . . c . . oh . . .f**** it just go out and beat them.'

What Ramsey did not know was how physical and tough the Yugoslavs would be. The World Champions were kicked and butted in front of a passionate 40,000 crowd. The Spanish referee quickly lost control and it was soon a war with little football played.

The Yugoslavs did not like Norman Hunter's early challenge on Osim and began to throw themselves down in blatant play acting in an effort to get an England player sent-off.

> ### The world champions were kicked and butted in front of a passionate 40,000 crowd.

England's outstanding performer was Alan Ball. He skipped and jumped over the tackles and the Yugoslavs could not hold him. Twice Ball opened up chances and Bobby Charlton went very close to putting England ahead. After 86 minutes Yugoslavia scored and there was more drama to follow with Mullery's sending off. Trivic chopped him down from behind and Mullery's fuse exploded. Fed up with being continually fouled, he spun round and retaliated and was dismissed, much to the delight of the home crowd and players. 'It was a diabolical foul,' said Mullery. 'I should not have retaliated but some of the things that went on that night, that were not punished, were incredible.'

ENGLAND 0 REPUBLIC OF IRELAND 1

12 June, 1988. Neckar Stadium,
Stuttgart, West Germany.

England Team: Shilton, Stevens, Sansom, Webb (Hoddle 60), Adams, Wright, Robson, Beardsley (Hateley 83), Lineker, Barnes, Waddle.

This was the biggest upset England has suffered in the European finals. The stadium was a sea of emerald green and the war of words had added to the atmosphere. The Irish had nothing to lose, England had everything. And they did.

England were the favourites and dominated long periods of the game. Paddy Bonner, in the Irish goal, made superb saves, particularly from Gary Lineker. Ireland had their fantastic spirit and the inspiration that was Jack Charlton. He used Ray Houghton and Tony Galvin to nullify the wide threat of John Barnes and Tony Waddle and it worked like a dream for him.

I can still see Glenn Hoddle, sitting on the ground by the England dug-out, legs outstretched, arms by his side, hardly watching the game. His body language was of a player who did not like being sub. His dark mood reflected England's performance.

The Irish goal came after just 20 minutes. Mark

IRISH JIG... England were never allowed to settle in Stuttgart and were later bundled out of the Championships.

The stadium was a sea of emerald green... The Irish had nothing to lose, England had everything. And they did.

Wright had a chance to clear, so did Kenny Sansom. The Arsenal full back's attempted clearance ballooned into the air, John Aldridge helped it on and Houghton headed in the most memorable goal of his life, the ball soaring up and over Peter Shilton.

'I will remember that goal and that match as long as I live,' said Houghton.

England staged a bombardment of the Irish goal. Hoddle came on to go close and Lineker and Peter Beardsley continued to miss chances. One Bonner save from Lineker late on was superb.

Afterwards the Irish drank their black velvet, sang and danced. England called for manager Bobby Robson to go and held an inquest. It reflected the different pressure England are always under.

England went on to lose all three group matches and travelled home in disgrace.

ENGLAND 1 SWEDEN 2

17 June, 1992. Rasunda Stadium,
Solna, Sweden.

England Team: Woods, Batty, Pearce, Keown, Walker, Palmer, Daley, Webb, Platt, Lineker (Smith 61) Sinton (Merson 76).

The Turnip was born. *The Sun* came out with one of its most famous headlines after this embarrassing and disastrous result. 'Swedes 2 Turnips 1' it screamed. Written by sports desk sub editor Dave Clement, the Turnip nickname stuck with manager Graham Taylor and eventually hounded him out of the job.

This match was also Gary Lineker's last for England. It ended in humiliation with Taylor

'SUB' STANDARD... Taylor was heavily criticised for his substitution of Lineker in Sweden.

substituting him for Alan Smith in the 64th minute. Taylor never lived it down as Lineker was public property. 'How could you treat a national hero like that?' was the debate.

England had taken the lead through David Platt. It was England's first goal in three matches in the Sweden finals and gave us hope. It should have been 3-0 in the first half but Tony Daley missed two sitters.

At half time Sweden sent on Ekstrom for Limpar and went long and high in the second half. They were the tactics that Taylor used so well at Watford but England could not cope.

Eriksson equalised and eight minutes from the end Brolin scored a superb winner for the Swedes. It was the goal of the tournament and brought huge celebration in Sweden, and more inquests and questions for the English.

Our record at all the European finals, apart from Euro 96, is desperate.

Taylor had started the tournament by saying to the fans at home 'Put your feet up, relax and let me do the worrying.' He was the worried one as he went home. Taylor survived but could not get England to the 1994 World Cup and it was all over for The Turnip.

ENGLAND 4 HOLLAND 1

18 June, 1996. Wembley Stadium.

England Team: Seaman, G.Neville, Pearce, Ince (Platt 68), Adams, Southgate, McManaman, Gascoigne, Shearer (Fowler 75), Sheringham (Barmby 75), Anderton.

One of England's finest results and performances, not only in the European Championships but in our history.

WALLOP!... Shearer belts in the third goal against the helpless Dutch.

UNBELIEVABLE... Sheri nets the fourth and Holland are buried.

It certainly represented the greatest night in the career of coach Terry Venables.

Holland, the masters of fantasy football in Europe and exponents of how the game should be played, were swept aside. In eleven breathtaking second-half minutes England scored three times.

Wembley was alive with atmosphere and never before has the famous old stadium celebrated so much. The Stadium of legends. It was a stadium of dreams that night.

Venables had told everyone to judge him when it mattered, during the finals.

And how right he was. It was not just the victory, it was the way England played.

We had taken the lead with Alan Shearer's penalty after Paul Ince had been brought down. No one could imagine what was to follow.

> I can still see Venables now, standing on the platform in the mixed zone area in the Wembley tunnel, smiling like a cat with the cream.

Teddy Sheringham headed in a Paul Gascoigne corner and then Sheringham unselfishly set up Shearer for number three. The SAS partnership was in full flow. There was more magic from Gazza. Number three in this spell and four on the night fell to Sheringham after Darren Anderton's shot rebounded to him.

Wembley went berserk and the Dutch were shell-shocked. Their consolation goal in the 77th minute from

WHAT A START!...Shearer heads England into an early lead.

Patrick Kluivert was significant. It kept them in the competition.

I can still see Venables now, standing on the platform in the mixed zone area in the Wembley tunnel, smiling like a cat with the cream. 'Yes, my greatest moment,' he said. 'Everything came together and this is how I always thought an England side, my England side, should play.'

ENGLAND 1 GERMANY 1
(Germany win 6-5 on penalties after extra time)
26 June, 1996. Wembley Stadium.

England Team: Seaman, Adams, Southgate, Pearce, Ince, Platt, Gascoigne, McManaman, Shearer, Sheringham, Anderton.

There are nights, matches and England games that will live in the memory forever. Diego Maradona's Hand Of God goal, England's penalty drama defeat in the semi-final of the 1990 World Cup, the World Cup defeat against Argentina with all its David Beckham drama . . . and this one.

What tension, what amazing scenes, what a story, what heartbreak … it was one of those nights that had everything. The old enemy and another penalty shoot out. Here was a game that left you feeling drained. I can remember going home and staying up for hours with a bottle of wine, cursing, recalling, kicking every ball. If you cared you had to be affected by this night.

There was real expectancy in the air and the place erupted when Tony Adams touched on Paul

Gascoigne's corner for Alan Shearer — who else in this tournament — to head England ahead.

The Germans were level after 16 minutes when Kuntz slid in at the far post.

Then deadlock. Two proud nations battling it out and no breakthrough.

Extra time was incredible. For the first time at a major tournament there was the golden goal rule. Who scored first went through to the final. Darren Anderton hit an upright and Gazza just failed to connect at the far post as England went within inches of reaching the second final in their history.

Penalties. Not again? It was 5-5 when Gareth Southgate trudged forward. 'Has he taken one before?' someone shouted. 'Yes, once, and he missed,' was the answer. Fingers crossed, legs crossed. The nation waited. You could hear a pin drop despite the 75,862 crowd. The rest is history. Southgate missed, Germany scored, as usual, and England were out.

Southgate, to his credit, held a press conference afterwards and apologised to the nation. He didn't have to. The saddest man at Wembley was undoubtedly Venables. This proved to be his last match in control because of behind-the-scenes problems with his business affairs and lack of support, he thought, from the FA's International Committee.

It could only happen in England. A great coach, someone the players respected, allowed to slip through the net.

DEJECTION...Gareth Southgate is inconsolable after his penalty miss handed Germany a place in the final.

Franz Beckenbauer
GERMANY

Date of birth: 11 September 1945
Clubs: Bayern Munich, New York Cosmos
International debut: 26 September 1965 v Sweden
International appearances: 103 (14 goals)

One of the greatest players of all time and certainly the finest defender ever seen. The ice-cool German, known as 'Der Kaiser', virtually invented the role of attacking sweeper which revolutionised the game during the 1970s.

Beckenbauer won every honour going during an unrivalled 28-year playing career and captained his country to European Championship glory in 1972. It was his first winners' medal at international level after being part of the German team beaten by England in the 1966 World Cup Final. But it certainly wasn't his last. Two years after that Euro final triumph against Russia in the Heysel Stadium, Beckenbauer lifted the World Cup in his home city of Munich.

Bayern Munich's captain when they won the European Cup three years in succession between 1974 and 1976, he was twice voted European Footballer of the Year. He retired as a player with New York Cosmos in 1984, and became the only man to win the World Cup as captain and manager when he took charge of his country's successful campaign in 1990. A master tactician, he is now the president of the German FA and a magnificent ambassador for his country's game.

Igor Belanov
USSR

Date of birth: 25 September 1960
Clubs: Dynamo Kiev, Borussia Moenchengladbach
International debut: 2 May 1985 v Switzerland
International appearances: 33 (9 goals)

The brilliant Soviet playmaker who was the mastermind behind his country's charge to the final of Euro 88 in Germany. In the end it needed the combined brilliance of Holland's Marco Van Basten and Ruud Gullit to halt the Russians. But Belanov's pace and probing passes, alongside midfield partner Alexander Zavarov, were the key to the Soviet's shock first round victories over the Dutch and a demoralised England. Had the Netherlands not lost to the Soviets in their opening game of the tournament, it is doubtful that they would have known how to cope with Belanov when they met again in the final 13 days later.

Born in Odessa, Belanov was transferred to the all-conquering Dynamo Kiev after just one season with his local club Chernomorets. His influence on the team was immediate and in 1986 Kiev became the last Soviet team to win a European trophy when they overwhelmed Atletico Madrid 3-0 in the Cup-Winners' Cup final. Voted European Footballer of the Year in 1986, Belanov was unfortunate to be at his peak while the Iron Curtain was still firmly in place, denying him the opportunity to export his talents to a wider European audience.

Giacinto Facchetti
ITALY

Date of birth: 18 July 1942
Clubs: Trevigliese, Internazionale
International debut: 27 March 1963 v Turkey
International appearances: 94 (3 goals)

Paul Gascoigne
ENGLAND

Date of birth: 27 May 1967
Clubs: Newcastle, Tottenham, Lazio, Rangers, Middlesbrough
International debut: 14 September 1988 v Denmark
International appearances: 57 (10 goals)

Famed Italian captain whose pace, strength and commitment made him a key figure when his country lit up Rome's Olympic Stadium by beating Yugoslavia in the replayed European Championship final of 1968.

An attacking left-back who scored 59 goals for Inter Milan during his career which spanned more than 17 years at the San Siro. Remarkably, Facchetti was naturally right footed and signed for Inter in 1960 as a striker. Yet his conversion to a left-sided defender paid immediate dividends and within two years he had won the first of a then-record 94 caps for Italy. A member of the Inter teams which won the European Cup in 1964 and 1965, he also won five Italian Championships and participated at three World Cup finals. A crucial member of the national squad when Italy reached the 1970 World Cup final against Brazil, he played in the next twelve internationals and was 35 when he won his final cap in 1977.

England's most talented player of the past decade...and also the most self-destructive. Gascoigne's failure to fulfil his incredible potential has been one of football's saddest spectacles. The memory of his magical moments makes his decline all the harder to swallow.

Gazza was just 23 when he became a national obsession on the back of his performances and his tears at Italia 90. It should have been the

Alain Giresse
FRANCE

Date of birth: 2 September 1952
Clubs: Bordeauux, Marseille
International debut: 23 April 1977 v Switzerland
International appearances: 47 (6 goals)

If Michel Platini was the undisputed star of Euro 84, Alain Giresse was the king-maker. It was the tireless midfield running of the tiny Giresse which allowed Platini the opportunity to shine so spectacularly in front of his own supporters.

Giresse was rapidly approaching his 32nd birthday at the start of those Championships, yet all of France knew that his motor and eye for an opening would be essential if the host nation were to triumph in the Parc des Princes. He didn't let them down. Ten years after making his debut for the French national team, Giresse took control of a midfield also boasting the talents of Jean Tigana and Luis Fernandez. He even weighed in with a rare international goal in the 5-0 thrashing of Belgium in Nantes, the result which convinced the rest of Europe that France were genuine title contenders.

Giresse, who spent most of his career with Bordeaux before bowing out with Marseille, played almost 600 French League games. He won 47 French caps in all, but it was his contribution to Euro 84 which guarantees him a free drink in every bar in France.

springboard to the stars but proved to be little more than a platform for his immaturity. Blessed with incredible balance and a God-given talent to spot a pass, he was in a class of his own as an attacking midfielder with Newcastle and then Spurs. But a reckless challenge in the 1991 FA Cup final signalled the start of a run of serious injuries which have blighted his career. An ill-fated move to Lazio failed to calm his wild spirit and many critics were calling for his omission from the 1996 European Championships after an infamous Hong Kong booze-up on the eve of the finals. But Terry Venables, who had signed Gascoigne for Spurs eight years previously, refused to bow to public pressure. And he was rewarded with one of the goals of the tournament when Gazza lobbed the ball over Scotland defender Colin Hendry, nipped round his beaten opponent and smashed a volley past keeper Andy Goram.

Ruud Gullit
HOLLAND

Date of birth: 1 September 1962
Clubs: Haarlem, Feyenoord, PSV Eindhoven, Milan, Sampdoria, Milan, Chelsea
International debut: 1 September 1981 v Switzerland
International appearances: 64 (17 goals)

Charismatic all-rounder who rivalled Diego Maradona as the world's finest footballer during the 1980s. Ten years after the departure of Cruyff, Neeskens and Krol, Gullit's emergence heralded a new generation of Dutch superstars who reached their peak at the 1988 European Championships.

At home in defence, midfield or attack, the powerfully-built Gullit honed his talents at Haarlem, Feyenoord and PSV Eindhoven before a world record £5.5 million transfer to AC Milan in 1987. Within a year he had won Euro 88, the Italian Championship and both the World and European Footballer of the Year awards. He scored twice in the European Cup Final against Steaua Bucharest in 1989 and collected another European Cup winners' medal and two further Italian Championships before moving to Sampdoria.

His arrival at Chelsea in 1995 signalled the start of an exciting new era for the London club, with dozens more top Euro stars following him to English football. A football genius whose intolerance of lesser talents was often mistaken for arrogance, he is currently back in Holland planning the next stage of his career after tempestuous spells as manager of Chelsea and Newcastle.

Jurgen Klinsmann
GERMANY

Date of birth: 30 September 1964
Clubs: Stuttgarter Kickers, VfB Stuttgart, Internazionale, Monaco, Tottenham, Bayern Munich, Sampdoria, Tottenham
International debut: 12 December 1987 v Brazil
International appearances: 108 (47 goals)

A clinical marksman whose retirement two years ago is still sorely felt by the Germans. A classic goal poacher who thrived on the big occasion, he trawled the European leagues in search of new experiences as well as big pay cheques.

From the moment Klinsmann finished his first season in senior football as second top scorer in the Bundesliga, it was apparent that he was a special talent. Acceleration, awareness and breathtaking close control made Klinsmann a nightmare for defenders to subdue. But it was his ability to be in the right place at the right time which marked him apart from other strikers.

Made his German debut in 1987 and was the star of their 1990 World Cup triumph, when they beat Argentina in a bad-tempered final. He also played at three European Championship finals, scoring in them all and lifting the trophy after the golden goal victory over the Czech Republic at the final of Euro 96. Played for Stuttgart, Inter Milan and Monaco before a shock move to Spurs in 1994. He was best known in England for his penalty box theatrics until his brilliant first season in the Premiership, when he was voted Footballer of the Year.

Sandro Mazzola
ITALY

Date of birth: 7 November 1942
Clubs: Internazionale
International debut: 12 May 1963 v Brazil
International appearances: 70 (22 goals)

Stylish striker whose flair and speed made him virtually unique in Italian football during the days when it was fashionable to twist and turn in the box, beat opponents time and again and pass the ball into the net. Mazzola was almost destined to become an Italian legend and few moments in football match his part in their European Championship triumph of 1968 for poignancy.

Mazzola was just six years old when his father Valentino, the captain of the Italian national side, was killed in the 1949 Torino air disaster. From the moment young Alessandro signed for Inter Milan in 1961, his career was obsessively monitored by the football crazy Italians. The attention was almost smothering, but the kid coped magnificently. Within two years of his debut for Inter, he won the first of 70 caps for the national side.

Although he did not make the team for the European Championship final against Yugoslavia, Mazzola was not to be denied his moment. A 1-1 draw in Rome's Olympic Stadium signalled the tournament's only replayed final. Mazzola was one of five changes to the team and his presence made all the difference as Italy won 2-0.

Gerd Muller
GERMANY

Date of birth: 3 November 1945
Clubs: Bayern Munich, Fort Lauderdale Strikers
International debut: 12 October 1966 v Turkey
International appearances: 62 (68 goals)

Sensational finisher whose goals won the World Cup and European Championships for his country, helping him become the first German to be voted European Footballer of the Year.

Short and squat with huge thighs, 'Der Bomber' was the most unlikely looking superstar of his generation. Bayern Munich coach Tschik Cajkovski moaned: 'I can't put that little elephant among my string of thoroughbreds,' when Muller was signed from Nordlingen in 1964. But he quickly changed his opinion of his new striker, who eventually netted an incredible 628 career goals including a Bundesliga record of 365.

Muller's international achievements were no less remarkable. At the 1970 World Cup finals he scored ten times, including two hat-tricks, to help Germany to the semi-finals. At the 1972 European Championships, he scored both goals against Belgium in the semi-finals and two more in the 3-0 win over the USSR. His most famous strike, though, was reserved for the finale — the World Cup final winner against Holland in Munich's Olympic Stadium. His 68 goals in 62 games for Germany remain a record unlikely to be surpassed.

Gunter Netzer
GERMANY

Date of birth: 14 September 1944
Clubs: Borussia Moenchengladbach, Real Madrid, Grasshopper
International debut: 9 October 1965 v Austria
International appearances: 37 (6 goals)

Twenty-eight years after the event, the name of Gunter Netzer still haunts English football. Not since Ferenc Puskas inspired Hungary's legendary victory of 1953 had a visiting player made a greater impression at Wembley than Netzer managed in April 1972.

England, still smarting over their World Cup defeat by the Germans two years earlier, were determined to

Antonin Panenka
CZECHOSLOVAKIA

Date of birth: 2 December 1948
Clubs: Bohemians, Rapid Vienna
International debut: 26 September 1973 v Scotland
International appearances: 60 (17 goals)

The midfield marvel with the droopy moustache who inspired a thousand imitators with his winning penalty in the 1976 shoot-out. Nobody held out much hope for the Czechs at that year's Championships, despite the fact that they finished a point ahead of England in their qualifying group to reach the last eight. Panenka's only contribution to those group games had been a hat-trick in the 4-0 rout of Cyprus, yet he proclaimed: 'No one expected us to do anything, so we simply resolved not to disgrace ourselves.'

Victory over the USSR and then Holland showed that Jozef Venglos' team were indeed no pushovers, yet their run was widely expected to come to an abrupt end in the Belgrade final against the mighty Germans. Czechoslovakia, though, had not read the script and raced into a 2-0 lead with goals from Svehlik and Dobias. Even when the Germans stormed

set the record straight in the first leg of their European Championship quarter-final. Germany, in their first return to Wembley since the 1966 World Cup, had other ideas. And Netzer had more ideas than most. The long-haired Borussia Moenchengladbach midfielder simply tormented Sir Alf Ramsey's team. Even Norman Hunter and Alan Ball couldn't get near him as Netzer scored from the spot and set up further goals for Hoeness and Muller in a crushing 3-1 victory. Having ousted German favourite Wolfgang Overath from the side, Netzer was at his peak that year, the key figure in Germany's European Championship triumph.

Twice German Footballer of the Year, he won the Bundesliga twice and added two Spanish Championships after a move to Real Madrid in 1974.

back through Dieter Muller and a last minute equaliser from Bernd Holzenbein, the Czechs were not to be denied. When Uli Hoeness missed from the spot, Panenka only had to net to land the title. His nerveless chip over the stranded Sepp Maier sent Europe crazy.

Michel Platini
FRANCE

Date of birth: 21 June 1955
Clubs: Nancy, St Etienne, Juventus
International debut: 27 March 1976 v Czechoslovakia
International appearances: 72 (41 goals)

One of the finest French players in history and the only man to be named European Footballer of the Year three years running. As an attacking midfielder, Platini was in a class of his own. In 72 appearances for France — 48 of which came as captain — he scored 41 times. For Juventus he finished top scorer in the Italian League on three separate occasions and netted the winning penalty in the tragic 1985 European Cup final against Liverpool.

Yet it was at international level that Platini really did the business. And no individual has ever dominated a European Championships more than Platini in 1984. In France's three first round games, he netted seven times, including hat-tricks against Belgium and Yugoslavia. He was on target again in the 3-2 semi-final defeat of Portugal in Marseilles, one of the greatest matches ever witnessed. And, of course, he netted the opening goal in the 2-0 final win over Spain to send Paris delirious.

Platini was just six days past his 29th birthday when he won the European Championships, yet just three years later he shocked football by announcing his retirement. When France built their magnificent new national stadium to stage the 1998 World Cup final, they wanted to name it the Stade de Platini. Typically, the great man declined the honour.

Luigi Riva
ITALY

Date of birth: 7 November 1944
Clubs: Cagliari
International debut: 26 June 1965 v Hungary
International appearances: 42 (35 goals)

Tall, rangy striker whose direct style made him one of the most popular players in Italian history. Remarkably, Riva achieved superstardom in football's most obsessive nation without ever signing for the giants of Juventus or Milan. In fact, he spent his entire career with the unfashionable Sardinian club of Cagliari, joining them when they were in the second division and remaining there 14 years until forced into a premature retirement by injuries. Even though he was the highest paid player in Italy during his peak, he turned down considerably more lucrative offers from Juve.

A converted left-winger, Riva steered Cagliari to promotion to Serie A in his first season in senior football. He made his international debut in 1965 but didn't hold a regular pace in the Azzuri for another two years. Guaranteed his place among Italian legends when he scored the opening goal in the replayed 1968 European Championship final against Yugoslavia in Rome. Riva scored a record 35 goals in 42 games for his country, including a goal against West Germany which helped Italy reach the 1970 World Cup final.

Karl-Heinz Rummenigge
GERMANY

Date of birth: 25 September 1955
Clubs: Lippstadt, Bayern Munich, Internazionale, Servette
International debut: 6 October 1976 v Wales
International appearances: 95 (45 goals)

The Golden Boy of Europe during the early 1980s, this powerful goalscorer captained his country to two World Cup finals and was twice named Europe's Footballer of the Year. Yet Rummenigge was more of a right-winger than a conventional striker, creating as many chances for the likes of Allofs, Voller and Hrubesch as he scored.

He was only 19 years old and still working as a bank clerk when Bayern Munich signed him from his home town club of Lippstadt and he proved an instant hit with Germany's most powerful club. Announced his arrival on the international stage at the 1978 World Cup finals in Argentina and was the fulcrum of the team which won the 1980 European Championships — supplying the corner for Horst Hrubesch's injury-time winner against Belgium in the final.

Captain of the German team which reached the World Cup Finals of 1982 and 1986, he joined Inter Milan for £2 million in 1984 and finished his career with Swiss club Servette. In total he made 95 appearances for his country, scoring 45 goals.

Peter Schmeichel
DENMARK

Date of birth: 18 November 1963
Clubs: Hvidore, Brondby, Manchester United, Sporting Lisbon
International debut: 10 May 1988 v Hungary
International appearances: 118

Alan Shearer
ENGLAND

Date of birth: 13 August 1970
Clubs: Southampton, Blackburn, Newcastle
International debut: 19 February 1992 v France
International appearances: 57 (28 goals)

The world's best goalkeeper for the best part of a decade, Schmeichel is still vital to Denmark's European Championship ambitions at the age of 36. The giant Dane was virtually unknown outside his home country until Manchester United signed him from Brondby for £500,000 in 1991. But within a year he was the talk of world football as he kept out the Dutch and then the Germans to help Denmark complete the greatest European Championship shock of the tournament's history.

A former newspaper advertising salesman, Schmeichel thrived on the full-time training at Old Trafford and emerged as a formidable last barrier as well as a fierce competitor. Courageous beyond the call of duty and blessed with magnificent agility and reflexes for such a big man, Schmeichel had no obvious faults. During eight years in English football he helped establish United as the most powerful club in the world. He won five League Championships, three FA Cups and the League Cup before captaining the team to a dramatic European Cup final victory in his last United appearance last year. Now playing in Portugal with Sporting Lisbon.

One of the most consistent scorers in the world today with nearly 300 career goals and plenty more still to come. England's qualifying form for Euro 2000 is hardly likely to worry any of their rivals in Belgium and Holland, but in Shearer, Kevin Keegan has a player who demands respect and can scare the life out of opponents.

From the moment he marked his first full game for Southampton with a hat-trick against Arsenal, Shearer has been a phenomenal finisher. He scored on his England debut against France in 1992 and soon proved he was a more than capable striking replacement for Gary Lineker. Despite a number of career-threatening injuries, Shearer has never lacked self-belief and cemented his reputation as Europe's finest striker with five goals in as many games as England reached the semi-finals of Euro 96.

At domestic level, he has twice handled the pressure of breaking the British transfer record. Indeed, his £15 million move from Blackburn to his home club Newcastle shortly after Euro 96 made him the world's costliest player.

Luis Suarez
SPAIN

Date of birth: 2 May 1935
Clubs: Deportivo La Coruna, Barcelona, Internazionale
International debut: 30 January 1957 v Holland
International appearances: 32 (14 goals)

Marco Van Basten
HOLLAND

Date of birth: 31 October 1964
Clubs: Ajax Amsterdam, Milan
International debut: 7 September 1983 v Iceland
International appearances: 58 (24 goals)

The devastating Dutchman scored one of the greatest goals in international history before his career was cruelly ended by a series of ankle injuries at the age of 28. Van Basten's incredible angled volley against the USSR in the final of Euro 88 was a fitting finish to an incredible tournament for the well-built striker. His five goals in five starts included a devastating hat-trick against England and was enough to earn him the first of his three European Footballer of the Year awards.

Signed by Ajax after being spotted at their youth talent 'gala', he scored the winning goal in the 1987 European Cup-Winners' Cup final against Lokomotiv Leipzig and also won three Dutch Championships and three Dutch Cups before a £1.5 million move to AC Milan in 1987. Struck up an immediate understanding with fellow Dutchman Ruud Gullit at the San Siro and together they turned Milan into Europe's most dominant club.

Van Basten scored twice when Milan thrashed Steaua Bucharest 4-0 in the 1989 European Cup final before his suspect ankles started to restrict his appearances. Forced to retire in 1993.

Dashing inside-forward who became one of the first players to capitalise on football's growing economic opportunities when he moved from Barcelona to Inter Milan in 1961. A skilful and industrious player, Suarez was blessed with visionary passing ability which marked him out as a prodigious goal maker as well as taker.

Signed by Barcelona in 1953 at the age of 18, he spent eight years at the Nou Camp and helped the club win the inaugural European Fairs Cup Final in 1958, when Barcelona thrashed a London representative side 8-2 on aggregate. Voted European Footballer of the Year in 1960, Suarez' greatest successes came in Milan, where he won three Italian Championships and the European Cup in 1964 and 1965.

At international level, his 32 appearances for Spain were spread over an extraordinary 15 year period, with his final cap coming at the age of 37. A member of the Spanish side which won the 1964 European Nations' Cup with a 2-1 victory over the USSR in the final, he was appointed Spanish national coach in 1988 after spells in charge of Italian clubs Genoa and Cagliari.

part in his final match for Dynamo in 1971. The following day he was appointed club coach but died of stomach cancer in March 1990 at the age of 60.

Dino Zoff
ITALY
Date of birth: 28 February 1942
Clubs: Udinese, Mantova, Napoli, Juventus
International debut: 20 April 1968 v Bulgaria
International appearances: 112

Current Italian coach who won the European Championships within two months of making his international debut then lifted the World Cup 14 years later.

Zoff was a late developing goalkeeper who didn't gain his first Italian cap until the age of 26, a year after joining Napoli from Mantova. Although he held onto the keeper's shirt for Euro 68, when Italy won the replayed final against Yugoslavia in Rome, he didn't truly establish himself as his country's undisputed number one for another four years when he transferred to Juventus. Thrived on the responsibility of playing for Italy's biggest club, winning five Italian Championships and the 1977 UEFA Cup.

In 1974 he established a world record when he played in 12 consecutive international games without conceding a goal. His proudest moment came in 1982 when he captained Italy to glory in the World Cup final four months after his 40th birthday. Finally retired in 1983 after 112 games for his country, he moved into coaching in 1988 when he was appointed in charge of team affairs at Juventus. Moved on to Lazio in 1993 and succeeded Cesare Maldini as national coach after the 1998 World Cup.

Lev Yashin
USSR
Date of birth: 22 October 1929
Clubs: Moscow Dynamo
International debut: 8 September 1954 v Sweden
International appearances: 78

Legendary Russian goalkeeper who was the star of his country's triumph at the inaugural European Nations' Cup in 1960. Dubbed 'the Black Panther' because of his famous all-black kit, Yashin's incredible agility and reflexes took the art of goalkeeping to new heights in the early 1960s.

Yet, remarkably, he did not even start playing football until the age of 22 and was originally signed by Moscow Dynamo as the netminder for their ice hockey team. Within two years of turning his attention to football, he won the first of his 78 caps for the USSR, earning a gold medal at the 1956 Olympics in Melbourne. Voted European Footballer of the Year in 1963 — still the only goalkeeper to win the award — he played in three successive World Cup finals for the USSR before announcing his international retirement in 1967.

Awarded the Order of Lenin by the Soviet government in 1968. Pele, Eusebio, Bobby Charlton and Franz Beckenbauer all flew to Moscow to take

DID YOU KNOW?

The fastest ever goal scored by a substitute in the finals came on 9 June 1996 when Spanish substitute Alfonso Perez took the field after 73 minutes as a replacement for Guillermo Amor against Bulgaria at Elland Road, and with his first touch deflected a free-kick into the opposition net to equalise and make the final score a 1-1 draw.

The first championship final ever decided by the controversial 'Golden Goal' was won by Germany, who defeated the Czech Republic 2-1 with Oliver Bierhoff scoring the decisive goal in the 94th minute of the 1996 Wembley Final.

The only Final to be decided on penalties came in 1976 when Czechoslovakia beat West Germany 5-3 in the penalty shoot-out. The game had ended 2-2 after extra time.

The Soviet Union were the first country to appear in three tournament finals (1960, 1964 and 1970) following their 3-0 defeat by West Germany in Brussels on 18 June 1972.

Yugoslavia became the first side to have been defeated in two championship finals, when they were beaten 2-0 by Italy in Rome on 10 June 1968 in a replay.

Future World Cup-winning manager (Sir) Alf Ramsey's first game in charge of England was a Nations Cup round one second leg tie, which was lost 5-2 against France in Paris on 27 February 1963.

The first country to withdraw from a championship was Spain, who in the 1958-60 event gave the Soviet Union a walkover after a disagreement dating back to the Spanish Civil War.

The first country to qualify for the final stages on goal difference was Romania, who in the 1970-72 event tied with Czechoslovakia in Group One on nine points each, but Romania progressed with a two-goal better goal difference.

On 16 June 1976, Anton Ondrus of Czechoslovakia scored for both sides in the semi-final against Holland in Zagreb. He opened the scoring for the Czechs after 20 minutes but put through his own goal after 77 minutes. Czechoslovakia eventually won 3-1 after extra time.

The first ever play-off in the event came while the competition was still a knockout. In the first round of the 1962-64 event, Bulgaria and Portugal each won their home legs 3-1 and a play-off in Rome on 23 March 1963 was required, Bulgaria winning 1-0.

England's best-ever performances in the European Championships have seen them lose at the semi-final stage, in 1968 and 1996, to Yugoslavia and Germany respectively.

Holland's legendary Johann Cruyff scored a total of 12 European Championship goals, two in the 1966-68 event, five in 1970-72 and five in 1974-76.

Italy's first defeat on home soil in the Nations Cup came on 15 October 1983, when they were defeated 3-0 by Sweden.

The Czech Republic's first game after changing their name from Czechoslovakia in the European Championships was a 6-1 home win over Malta on 6 September 1994.

France's first three home Nations Cup ties yielded them 17 goals, a 7-1 win against Greece on 1 October 1958, a 5-2 win against Austria on 13 December 1959 and a 5-4 defeat by Yugoslavia in 1960.

Denmark's first game as defending European champions in the 1994-96 series was a 1-1 draw in Macedonia on 7 September 1994, the first ever game in the competition for the hosts.

Despite their earlier success in the competition, the first man to score a European Championships hat-trick in one game for Yugoslavia was Zlatro Vujovic, in a 4-0 victory against Turkey on 29 October 1986.

Slovenia's first ever away win in the European Championships came at the fourth attempt with a 3-1 win in Estonia on 11 June 1995.

Sweden's last European Championship defeat was a 2-1 loss to Turkey on 29 March 1995, and they are unbeaten in 12 games since.

The first man to referee a Nations Cup final was an Englishman, Arthur Ellis, who took charge at the July 1960 Soviet Union-Yugoslavia match at Parc des Princes in Paris.

The first man to appear as a substitute in a Nations Cup final was Oleg Dolmatov, a half-time replacement for Anatoli Konkov in the Soviet Union's 3-0 defeat in the 1972 Final.

West Germany's 1972 European Championships-winning side contained only two survivors from the team defeated in the 1966 World Cup Final, Franz Beckenbauer and Horst-Dieter Hottges.

West Germany's 1972 3-0 win against the Soviet Union remains the biggest margin of victory in any European Championship Final.

West Germany's 1972 quarter-final 3-1 win at Wembley against England was their first win at the historic stadium.

1964 European Championship-winning coach Jose Villalonga was no stranger to European success, having managed Real Madrid to their first European Cup successes in 1956 and 1957.

The only side ever to win a Nations Cup semi-final on the toss of a coin were Italy, who on 5 June 1978 defeated the Soviet Union after drawing 0-0 after extra time.

On 17 June 1976, West Germany's Dieter Muller became the first player to score a semi-final hat-trick, when his 80th, 114th and 119th minute goals helped his nation to a 4-2 win after extra time against Yugoslavia.

The 1980 event was the first to include eight countries in the finals series.

The only player to be dismissed in a European Championship Final was Yvon Le Roux of France, dismissed in the 84th minute of the 1984 Final at Parc des Princes, Paris.

The late call-up of subsequent surprise champions Denmark to the 1992 finals in Sweden forced coach Richard Moller Nielsen to put off his original summer task of decorating his kitchen.

With goals in the finals of 1988, 1992 and 1996, Jurgen Klinsmann is the only player to have scored in three finals tournaments.

The first 16-team European Championship finals were held in England in 1996.

⚽ The 1984 finals in France were the first not to feature a play-off for third and fourth place.

⚽ On 9 December 1987, the only 'behind closed doors' European Championship qualifier took place in Amsterdam when Holland defeated Cyprus 4-0. The original 8-0 win in Rotterdam in October was declared void after an orange thrown from the crowd hit visiting keeper Andreas Charitou.

⚽ Holland's 1992 20-man European Championship finals squad contained 18 players who had won major club honours in the 1991-92 season. Only Eric Viscaak (Gent) and Jan Wouters (Bayern Munich) came to the event without some sort of award.

⚽ Throughout the 1996 finals in England, Bulgarian Hristo Stoichkov was the only player to score direct from a free-kick (against France, 68 mins, 18 June 1996, lost 3-1).

⚽ The first finals game ever to feature a 'golden goal' period of extra time failed to produce one. The June 1996 England-Spain quarter-final ran its full course, ultimately to a penalty shoot-out.

⚽ On 20 April 1994, the tiny nation of Liechtenstein played in its first European Championship qualifying tie, a Group Six game in Belfast, which was lost 4-1 to Northern Ireland.

⚽ On 16 April 1975, Malcolm Macdonald scored all five goals in a 5-0 win against Cyprus at Wembley to become England's most prolific scorer in a single Nations Cup game.

⚽ Helmut Schoen, coach of the successful 1972 Championship-winning side, also guided his nation to the 1976 finals, where they lost the Final to Czechoslovakia after a penalty shoot-out.

⚽ The 1976 European Championship Final between Czechoslovakia and West Germany saw Franz Beckenbauer win his 100th international cap, having made his international debut in 1965.

⚽ 65-year-old West German Fritz Neuman of Frankfurt was so keen to see the opening game of the 1980 finals in Rome between Czechoslovakia and West Germany that he cycled 850 miles to Rome to watch the match.

⚽ Though they failed to qualify for the 1984 finals, Czechoslovakia's first goal in their home 2-2 draw against Sweden on 6 October 1982, scored by Petr Janecka, was the 100th scored by a Czech in the competition.

⚽ At Euro 96, there were four penalty shoot-outs, won by England (4-2 v Spain in the quarter-finals), France (5-4 v Holland in the quarter-finals), Germany (6-5 v England in the semi-finals) and the Czech Republic (6-5 v France in the semi-finals).

⚽ Euro 96 was the first European Championship finals at which attendances totalled over one million, with 1,268,201 spectators watching the 31 games at an average of 40,916 for each match.

⚽ The highest average attendance for a European Championship finals tournament is the 53,989 who saw each of the 15 games at the 1988 finals in Germany.

⚽ At Euro 96, 37 of the 42 penalties in the four shoot-outs were successful.

⚽ The top individual scorers at each Championship finals were: 1960: Galic (Yugoslavia), Heutte (France), Ivanov

(Soviet Union), Jerkovic (Yugoslavia) and Pondelnik (Soviet Union), two goals each. 1964: Bene (Hungary), Novak (Hungary) and Pereda (Spain), two goals each. 1968: Dzajic (Yugoslavia), two goals. 1972: Gerd Muller (West Germany) four goals. 1976: Dieter Muller (West Germany) four goals. 1980: Klaus Allofs (West Germany) three goals. 1984: Michel Platini (France) nine goals. 1988: Marco Van Basten (Holland) five goals. 1992: Bergkamp (Holland), Brolin (Sweden) and Riedle (Germany), Henrik Larsen (Denmark) three goals each. 1996: Shearer (England) five goals.

⚽ Marco Van Basten's hat-trick past England goalkeeper Peter Shilton ('celebrating' his 100th cap) in Holland's 3-1 win over England in Dusseldorf on 15 June 1988, was the first conceded by an English goalkeeper since 1959.

⚽ In Germany's 2-0 win over the Czech Republic on 9 June 1996, referee David Elleray showed his yellow card to ten players, the highest total in any one single match of the event.

⚽ The Russian squad at Euro 96 were given special dispensation to register their vote by fax in the general elections taking part in Russia during the tournament in England.

⚽ The first ever European Nations Championship qualifying tie was staged on 28 September 1958 in Moscow's Lenin stadium in front of a 100,572 crowd between the USSR and Hungary, which the home side won 3-1.

⚽ In the 1962-64 series, the France v England first round tie saw England employ different managers in each leg. Walter Winterbottom's last game in charge saw his side draw 1-1 at Hillsborough, but Alf Ramsey's debut as manager was soured by a 5-2 defeat in Paris.

⚽ The biggest ever attendance for a European Nations Cup tie was the 130,711 who packed Hampden Park to see the February 1968 match between Scotland and England, a 1-1 draw which was enough to secure qualification for the world champions.

⚽ The 1970-72 series of Nations Cup ties was the first in which two substitutions, rather than one, were allowed.

⚽ The 24 November 1975 Hungary v Austria meeting in Budapest was Hungary's 500th full international and the 120th meeting between the two sides. Hungary won 2-1. England's 3-0 victory in Salonika aganst Greece in a Group 3 qualifier on 17 November 1982 was Bobby Robson's first victory as England manager.

⚽ 49 countries entered the qualifying group stages of Euro 2000, the highest number yet, beating the 48 for Euro 96.

⚽ In the 1994-96 series, qualifying group four consisted of six countries, of whom only Italy had previously competed in the European Championships. Croatia, Estonia, Lithuania, Slovakia and Ukraine were all new to the competition.

⚽ On 20 September 1978, the Republic of Ireland and Northern Ireland met for the first time at full international level, sharing a 0-0 draw in front of 55,000 supporters at Dublin's Lansdowne Road.

⚽ Referees in European Championship Finals:
  – 1960: Ellis (England)
  – 1964: Holland (England)
  – 1968: (1st game) Dienst (Switzerland), (replay) Ortiz de Mendibil (Spain)
  – 1972: Marschall (Austria)
  – 1976: Gonella (Italy)
  – 1980: Rainea (Romania)
  – 1984: Christov (Czechoslovakia)
  – 1988: Vautrot (France)
  – 1992 Galler (Switzerland)
  – 1996 Pairetto (Italy)

⚽ Oliver Bierhoff's two goals for Germany in the 1996 Final against the Czech Republic made him the first substitute to score in a European Championship Final.

⚽ In the 1998-2000 series, Spain's Group 6 qualifying tally of 42 goals in eight games is the highest total ever recorded in qualifying.

UEFA's decision to award the Euro 2000 championships to both Belgium and Holland was based on the fact that neither country had eight venues large enough to stage the first major sporting event of the new millennium. So they have split the games — and the costs — down the middle. In theory, having two host nations can only complicate matters. In reality, though, the accessibility and excellent transport systems of the two countries offer supporters the chance to visit some of the most exciting cities in Europe.

AMSTERDAM ▲

One of the most vibrant cities in the world, the Dutch capital is famous for its bars, restaurants, bikes, culture … and its red light district. The entire city, dating back to the 17th century, is dominated by an intricate canal system running 50 miles throughout the central districts. The famous Rijksmuseum, the Van Gogh Museum and the many flea markets are all worth a visit, as are the 'Brown Bars' and the designated coffee shops with their relaxed smoking rules. Much of Amsterdam's nightlife revolves around the Leidseplein and Rembrandtsplein.

THE STADIUM: Amsterdam Arena

Ajax's futuristic home on the suddenly trendy south east side of Amsterdam was opened in 1996 and cost more than £80 million to build. With a 50,000 capacity, a sliding roof and restaurant and conference facilities, the club were hoping to stage the Euro 2000 final but found themselves outbid by Rotterdam. The complex also contains Ajax's famous youth academy headquarters, de Toekomst ('the future').

GETTING THERE: Dozens of daily flights from all major British cities. Schiphol Airport is a 20 minute train ride from Amsterdam's city centre. Eurostar from London Waterloo (change at Brussels) takes 7 ½ hours.

THE MATCHES: 11 June Holland v Czech Republic (Group D), 18 June Slovenia v Spain (Group C), 21 June France v Holland (Group D), 24 June Quarter-final 1 (winners Group A v runners up Group B), 29 June Semi-final 2.

ARNHEM ▶

Situated in the east of the country not far from the German border, Holland's fifth largest city was the scene of one of the fiercest battles of the Second World War, memorably relived by the film 'A Bridge Too Far'. The capital of the Gelderland province, Arnhem's night life centres around the pavement cafes of the Korenmarkt while the city's Hoge Veluwe National Park contains the world's largest collection of Van Goghs in the Kroller Muller Museum.

THE STADIUM: Gelredome

The most modern stadium in Europe, the Gelredome was ten years in the planning but did not open until 1998. The home to Vitesse Arnhem with a 26,000 capacity, it features a retractable roof weighing an incredible 800 tonnes. But it's the retractable pitch, encased in a giant frame which can be rolled through the stadium doors in a couple of hours by four computer-controlled hydraulic machines, which makes the stadium unique.

Three days after Vitesse's first game there, the pitch was removed to allow the Spice Girls to play a concert.

GETTING THERE: Arnhem is an hour's train ride from Amsterdam Central Station or Schiphol Airport and 90 minutes drive from the Dutch capital.
THE MATCHES: 11 June Turkey v Italy (Group B), 17 June Romania v Portugal (Group A), 21 June Slovenia v Norway (Group C).

BRUGES ▼

Europe's best preserved medieval city and the biggest tourist attraction in Belgium. The winding streets and meandering canals have earned Bruges the name of 'the Venice of the North' and the comparisons are clear. One of Europe's leading trade centres during the middle ages, the centre of the Flemish speaking city is still dominated by the 83-metre tall belfry tower which delivers spectacular views of the picturesque region.

THE STADIUM: Jan Breydel Stadium

The home of both Club Brugge and Cercle Brugge, the municipally owned Olympiastadion was built in 1975 when both teams ran into financial difficulties and decided that ground sharing was the only way to survive. A major refurbishment and expansion scheme has increased the capacity from 14,500 to 35,000, with the stadium being renamed after one of Flanders' medieval rebel leaders. A special match day bus service runs from the main train centre, ten minutes ride away.

GETTING THERE: Bruges is just ten miles away from the port of Ostend, which is a four-hour ferry ride from Dover. The Eurostar from London Waterloo also stops at Bruges station on the way to Brussels.

THE MATCHES: 11 June Denmark v France (Group D), 16 June Czech Republic v France (Group D), 21 June Yugoslavia v Spain (Group C), 25 June Quarter-final 4 (winners Group C v runners-up Group D).

BRUSSELS ▼

The capital of Belgium and administrative headquarters of the European Parliament, Brussels is one of the major business centres of the modern world. Yet it still has a proud heritage and culture dating back hundreds of years and its citizens are proud of the picturesque streets, the unique Grote Markt and the art nouveau design of many of their houses. Famous for the Atomium, beer and chocolate, but probably best known for the appropriately named statue of the Manneken Pis.

THE STADIUM: King Baudouin Stadium

Built on the site of the ill-fated Heysel Stadium, Belgium's new national stadium was opened in 1995, ten years after the infamous European Cup final when 39 died during fighting between Liverpool and Juventus fans. Although parts of the original ground still exist, the Belgian authorities have done everything possible to eradicate all memories of Heysel. The new purpose built stadium, with a 50,000 capacity, has its own train station at the end of Metro Line 1A, 20 minutes from the Gare du Midi.

GETTING THERE: Regular daily flights from Britain to Brussels Airport at Zavantem, ten miles to the north east of the city. Eurostar direct from London Waterloo takes just 2 hours and 40 minutes.

THE MATCHES: 10 June Belgium v Sweden (Group B), 14 June Italy v Belgium (Group B), 19 June Turkey v Belgium (Group B), 24 June Quarter-final 2 (winners Group B v runners-up Group A), 28 June Semi-final 1.

CHARLEROI ▶

The largest city in Belgium's French speaking region of Wallonia is 30 miles south of Brussels on the River Sambre. Established as a fortified town in 1666, it was named after Charles II of Spain, who was sovereign of the Spanish Netherlands at that time. The area became rich on the back of its coalmining industry during the 18th century. The city's economy is now based on steelmaking and glass.

THE STADIUM: Stade Communal

England's base for two of their Group A games, the Stade Communal features some of the steepest stands to be found at any European stadium, although UEFA are adamant they are perfectly safe. The home of Charleroi, originally built in 1904, has undergone a major facelift for Euro 2000 with three of the

pyramid-shaped stands being constructed within the last two years. As soon as the championships are finished, the third tier of the main stands will be removed, reducing the Stade Communal's capacity from 30,000 to 22,000.

GETTING THERE: Charleroi Brussels South Airport is just six miles from the city centre. Some direct flights from the UK or a 40-minute train ride from the more accessible Brussels International Airport.

THE MATCHES: 13 June Yugoslavia v Slovenia (Group C), 17 June England v Germany (Group A), 20 June England v Romania (Group A).

EINDHOVEN ▼

This dynamic young city in the south of the country is at the heart of Holland's technical revolution. The home of the giant Philips industrial and research plant as well as DAF and the International Centre of Technology, Eindhoven is also one of the most affluent cities, a fact reflected in the number of fashionable bars which have sprung up in the central streets of Kleine Berg and Stratumseind. One in five inhabitants of Eindhoven is employed by Philips — and they all support PSV.

THE STADIUM: Philips Stadium

More of a business and shopping complex than a football ground, PSV's home, like everything else in Eindhoven, owes everything to the electrical giants of Philips. Renovation of the 33,000 all-seater stadium started in 1988 and is still going on. Used 365 days a year for meetings, receptions and events, the ground features four huge video screens, two restaurants, a brasserie and a massive Toys R Us store. Oh yes, it also has rooftop gas heaters to keep the crowds warm in winter!

GETTING THERE: No direct flights from the UK to Eindhoven's small airport, but well served by modern motorway system and regular trains from Amsterdam Central and Schiphol Airport.

THE MATCHES: 12 June Portugal v England (Group A), 15 June Sweden v Turkey (Group B), 19 June Italy v Sweden (Group B).

LIEGE ▶

Picturesque university town to the east of Belgium, Liege is situated just 20 miles from the German border, close to Cologne. This French-speaking city, with 200,000 inhabitants, dates right back to medieval times and proudly boasts that it was in Liege that the Latin and Germanic worlds first came together in the 15th century. The palace of prince-bishops and the churches of St.Jacques and St.Barthelmey have all survived more than 500 years.

THE STADIUM: Sclessin Stadium
With its stands close to the pitch, the Sclessin was specifically modelled on English grounds when it was designed in 1984 in order to generate greater atmosphere from the crowds. A second phase of the ground, home to Standard Liege, was built in 1993 and the rebuilding for Euro 2000 was completed last year with a new stand on the side of the River Meuse and an extra tier on the main stand to create a capacity of 30,000.

GETTING THERE: There are no direct flights to Liege from Britain but the city is served by one of the best rail systems in the world, with regular trains from Brussels taking less than two hours.

THE MATCHES: 12 June Germany v Romania (Group A), 18 June Norway v Yugoslavia (Group C), 21 June Denmark v Czech Republic (Group D).

ROTTERDAM ▼

The second largest city in Holland and the biggest commercial port in the world, Rotterdam loves nothing better than putting one over on the capital city of Amsterdam. So you can imagine their delight when Rotterdam's city councillors persuaded UEFA to stage the Euro 2000 final at their Feyenoord Stadium. Rotterdam is a bustling, go-ahead city of some 600,000 inhabitants. It's impressive modern architecture includes the Erasmus Bridge across the Meuse, the impressive skylines and famous cubic houses.

THE STADIUM: Feyenoord Stadium
Fondly known as 'De Kuip' ('The Tub'), Feyenoord's home has been the Dutch national stadium since it was built in 1937. But they have had to work hard to preserve their status, with the superb new stadia in Amsterdam and Eindhoven threatening their special status. Although Rotterdam had hosted a record eight European finals, the ground had become shabby and was falling to pieces by the end of the 1980s. It needed

a massive financial injection from the Rotterdam city council to fund the complete overhaul which gives all 50,000 spectators an unobstructed view of the pitch.

GETTING THERE: Direct flights to Rotterdam from the UK, although many find it cheaper to fly to Amsterdam Schiphol and travel on the hourly train service to Rotterdam.

THE MATCHES: 13 June Spain v Norway (Group C), 16 June Denmark v Holland (Group D), 20 June Portugal v Germany (Group A), 25 June Quarter-final 3 (winners Group D v runners-up Group C), 2 July Final.

EURO 2000 TOURNAMENT PLANNER

Team	Venue	Date/Time
Group A		
Germany v Romania	Liège	12 June 5.00
Portugal v England	Eindhoven	12 June 7.45
Romania v Portugal	Arnhem	17 June 5.00
England v Germany	Charleroi	17 June 7.45
Portugal v Germany	Rotterdam	20 June 7.45
England v Romania	Charleroi	20 June 7.45
Winner: _____		**Runner-up:** _____
Group B		
Belgium v Sweden	Brussels	10 June 7.45
Turkey v Italy	Arnhem	11 June 1.30
Italy v Belgium	Brussels	14 June 7.45
Sweden v Turkey	Eindhoven	15 June 7.45
Turkey v Belgium	Brussels	19 June 7.45
Italy v Sweden	Eindhoven	19 June 7.45
Winner: _____		**Runner-up:** _____
Group C		
Spain v Norway	Rotterdam	13 June 5.00
Yugoslavia v Slovenia	Charleroi	13 June 7.45
Slovenia v Spain	Amsterdam	18 June 5.00
Norway v Yugoslavia	Liège	18 June 7.45
Yugoslavia v Spain	Bruges	21 June 5.00
Slovenia v Norway	Arnhem	21 June 5.00
Winner: _____		**Runner-up:** _____
Group D		
France v Denmark	Bruges	11 June 5.00
Holland v Czech Republic	Amsterdam	11 June 7.45
Czech Republic v France	Bruges	16 June 5.00
Denmark v Holland	Rotterdam	16 June 7.45
France v Holland	Amsterdam	21 June 7.45
Denmark v Czech Republic	Liège	21 June 7.45
Winner: _____		**Runner-up:** _____

Quarter-finals

Match 25
Amsterdam   24 June 5.00
Winners Group A v Runners-up Group B

WINNER _____

Match 26
Brussels   24 June 7.45
Winners Group B v Runners-up Group A

WINNER _____

Match 27
Rotterdam   25 June 5.00
Winners Group D v Runners-up Group C

WINNER _____

Match 28
Bruges   25 June 7.45
Winners Group C v Runners-up Group D

WINNER _____

Semi-finals

Match 29
Brussels   28 June 7.45
Winners Match 25 v Winners Match 28

WINNER _____

Match 30
Amsterdam   29 June 5.00
Winners Match 26 v Winners Match 27

WINNER _____

Final

Match 31
Rotterdam   2 July 7.00
Winners Match 29 v Winners Match 30

_____

Euro 2000 Champions

_____

Kick-off times (all pm) refer to BST. For local times, add one hour.